BLACK & DECKER®
HOME IMPROVEMENT LIBRARY ™

Exterior Home Repairs & Improvements

Cy DeCosse Incorporated
Minnetonka, Minnesota

Contents

Library of Congress
Cataloging-in-Publication Data

Exterior home repairs & improvements.

p. cm.—(Black & Decker home
improvement library)
Includes index.
ISBN 0-86573-744-4 (hardcover).
ISBN 0-86573-745-2 (softcover).
1. Dwellings—Maintenance and repair—
Amateurs' manuals. 2. Exterior walls—
Maintenance and repair—
Amateurs' manuals.
I. Cy DeCosse Incorporated.
II. Series.
TH4817.3.E948   1995
643'.7—dc20   95-12393

CY DeCOSSE INCORPORATED

A COWLES MAGAZINES COMPANY

Chairman/CEO: Bruce Barnet
Chairman Emeritus: Cy DeCosse
President/COO: Nino Tarantino
Executive V.P./Editor-in-Chief:
 William B. Jones

Created by: The editors of Cy DeCosse
Incorporated, in cooperation with Black
& Decker. BLACK&DECKER is a trademark
of the Black & Decker Corporation and
is used under license.

Project Director: Paul Currie
Project Manager: Ron Bygness
Senior Editor: Mark Johanson
Editors: Jim Huntley, John Mugford,
  Jon Simpson
Senior Art Director: Tim Himsel
Art Directors: John Hermansen,
  Geoffrey Kinsey, Gina Seeling
Technical Production Editors: Greg Pluth,
  Gary Sandin
Assistant Technical Production Editors:
  Dan Cary, Tom Heck
*Vice President of Development Planning &
  Production:* Jim Bindas
Copy Editor: Janice Cauley
Contributing Editors: Mark Biscan, Abby
  Gnagey, Carol Harvatin, Joel Schmarje,
  Bryan Trandem

Shop Supervisor: Phil Juntti
Set Builders: Jon Hegge, Troy Johnson,
  Rob Johnstone, John Nadeau
Sr. Production Manager: Laurie Gilbert
Production Staff: Willis Alexander, Deborah
  Eagle, Kevin Hedden, Jeanette Moss,
  Mike Schauer, Greg Wallace,
  Kay Wethern, Nik Wogstad
Director of Photography: Mike Parker
Creative Photo Coordinator:
  Cathleen Shannon
Studio Manager: Marcia Chambers
Lead Photographer: Charles Nields
Photographers: Rebecca Hawthorne,
  Rex Irmen, Mark Macemon,
  Paul Najlis

Contributing Photographers: Phil Aarrestad,
  Kim Bailey, Steve Smith
Contributing Photography: Airhawk
  Ventilation Products by The Solar Group;
  The Energy Conservatory; Infrared
  Inspections, Inc.; Orkin Pest Control;
  Skyview Photos of America, Inc.; Vande
  Hey Raleigh Architectural Roof Tile
  Company, Inc.
Contributing Model Builder: Glenn Terry

Printed on American paper by:
  R. R. Donnelley & Sons Co.
99 98 97 96 / 5 4 3 2 1

"Wire-Nut®" is a registered trademark of Ideal
Industries, Inc.

Introduction

The roof, windows, doors, and exterior walls of your house work together to create a shield that keeps your home healthy and protects your family from the elements. By adhering to a program of scheduled maintenance and inspection and making timely repairs and improvements, you can ensure that your home provides maximum enjoyment for you and your family, with a minimum of work and expense.

Exterior Home Repairs & Improvements shows you how to maintain the outside of your house by developing the ability to spot trouble and make repairs that improve the appearance and keep minor problems from becoming major headaches. Once you have determined a course of action to correct problems or make improvements, we give you clear instructions on how to accomplish the most common exterior home repairs and improvements.

This book begins with some helpful information on how to inspect the exterior of your home—what to look for, how to investigate beyond the surface, and where to look for solutions to any problems you detect. Then, we cover the basics of working safely outdoors and at heights. From there, the book is divided into five sections that give you further information on identifying and solving specific problems.

Roof Systems contains information on repairing roofs and flashing; reshingling a roof; repairing and replacing gutters, soffits and fascia; and adding roof and soffit vents.

Repairing Siding & Trim covers repairs for all the most common siding types: wood lap, vinyl, metal, stucco, shakes, and board-and-batten. It also contains instructions for repairing exterior trim.

Insulating & Weatherizing shows you how to analyze the energy efficiency of your home, and how to upgrade insulation and weatherstripping with the best products for the job.

Painting Your House gives you start-to-finish instructions that cover every aspect of the painting process. We discuss paint and painting materials, give thorough preparation instructions, and show you how to apply paint to the many different surfaces and materials you will find on the outside of your house.

Protecting & Maintaining Your Home concludes the book with a variety of exterior projects, from pestproofing to security, that create a safer, more pleasant living environment.

Use this book as a guide for making repairs and improvements to the exterior of your house, and for creating a regular exterior maintenance and evaluation program that will make future exterior projects less frequent and more manageable.

Inspecting Your House

Routine maintenance checks of the exterior of your house do not have to be time-consuming. If you know what to look for and where to look, a semi-annual inspection can be done in 30 minutes—an excellent investment when compared to the cost of fixing problems that could have been prevented with early detection.

By conducting your inspection in a logical sequence, you will save even more time. A good strategy is simply to start at the top, with the roof system, and work your way down and around the house, finishing up with your foundation, driveway, and sidewalks. Do not forget to make important interior inspections, like looking for water damage and checking insulation and weatherstripping.

To assist you in your inspections, we have included an exterior maintenance checklist and some helpful tips on the following pages. Also be sure to refer to the pages cited to the right as you make your evaluation. There, you will find helpful information on what to look for in specific areas of your house, as well as how to plan a strategy for correcting problems.

The following items are helpful when you inspect your house:
• An exterior house maintenance checklist (page 9)
• Binoculars
• A note pad and pencil

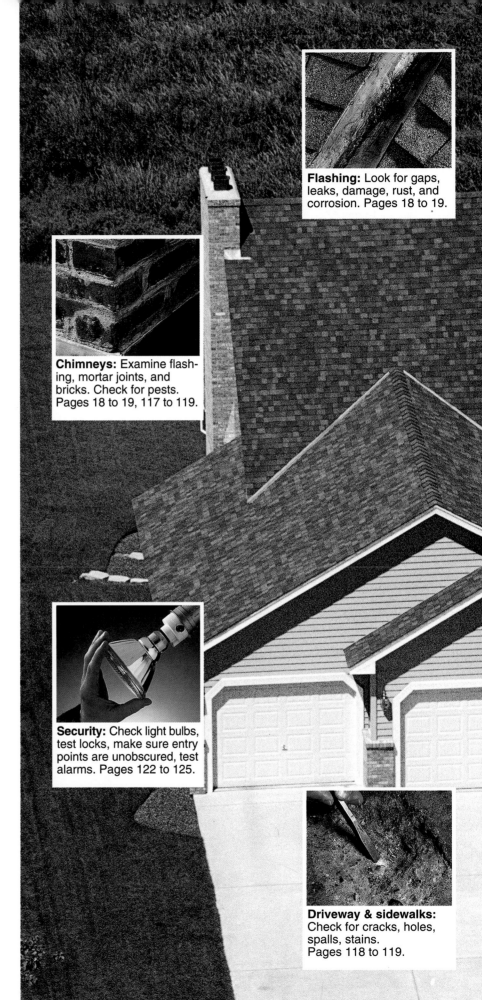

Flashing: Look for gaps, leaks, damage, rust, and corrosion. Pages 18 to 19.

Chimneys: Examine flashing, mortar joints, and bricks. Check for pests. Pages 18 to 19, 117 to 119.

Security: Check light bulbs, test locks, make sure entry points are unobscured, test alarms. Pages 122 to 125.

Driveway & sidewalks: Check for cracks, holes, spalls, stains. Pages 118 to 119.

Shingles: Inspect for buckling, cupping, wear, and damage.
Pages 18 to 19.

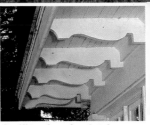

Soffits, fascia, & trim: Look for signs of rot, paint failure, and pests.
Pages 18 to 19, 58 to 59, 98 to 99.

Gutters & do
Check for lea
and clogs. Pa
18 to 19.

Siding: Look for paint failure, rot, popped nails, dirt buildup, gaps, missing sections. Pages 58 to 59, 72 to 73.

Windows & doors: Test for gaps, check paint, weatherstripping, and glass and screening. Pages 58 to 59, 72 to 73, 122 to 125.

Making scheduled inspections

Making scheduled inspections of the exterior of your house is an important responsibility. Make a photocopy of the exterior house maintenance checklist on the following page, and use it to help organize your inspections. Make a check in the box next to any problems you detect, and grade the general condition of each part of your house in the columns to the left.

In moderate and cold climates, inspect your house at least twice a year—once in the spring, and again in the fall. In spring, check to see how well your home weathered the winter. Look for signs of paint failure and damage or wear to your roof system. In the fall, check windows, doors, ventilation, and weatherstripping to make sure the house is well sealed. In warmer climates, it is not as important to divide your inspections into seasonal checkups. But heat and rain can be as harsh on the exterior of a house as ice, snow, and freezing temperatures, so be sure to make inspections at least once a year.

Tips for inspecting your house

• **Look beyond the surface** by probing damaged areas with an awl or a thin-blade screwdriver. Deteriorated wood in need of repair sometimes looks almost normal on the surface.

• **Use binoculars** instead of a ladder for a quick visual inspection of roofs, gutters, chimneys, and second-story areas. If you spot any potential problems, use a ladder for closer inspection (see pages 10 to 13 for tips on ladder safety).

• **Keep permanent records** of your inspection, noting any areas of concern. Monitor the areas carefully, and take action as soon as it becomes clear that a problem is developing.

• **Take photographs** of roofs, walls, and any other parts of your house showing signs of wear. Compare photos from year to year to determine the rate the wear is increasing. Significant changes within a year or two are a sure sign that a problem exists.

• **Check the grounds** near your house for trouble signs, like flakes of paint, roofing-material wash-off, or soil erosion.

Tips for Identifying the Source of a Moisture Problem

Shown cutaway for clarity

Moisture problems affect houses in all climates. Identifying the source of moisture problems can be tricky because the effects of moisture often appear far from the actual source. *Ice dams* (left) at roof eaves are a common occurrence in colder climates. They result from inadequate attic ventilation (pages 52 to 55), which causes snow to melt higher up the roof. The runoff then freezes when it comes in contact with the colder roof overhang. *Ceiling stains* (center) show up on interior surfaces, but often are caused by leakage from failed roof materials or flashing (pages 18 to 19). *Peeling paint* (right) can occur if your house was improperly prepared for paint, or if the paint was not applied correctly. More likely, there is a condensation problem caused by excess moisture inside the house, or a missing vapor barrier (pages 98 to 99).

Exterior House Maintenance Checklist   Date:

1	2	3	Roof, Gutters, Soffits & Fascia
			Shingles: ❏ buckling ❏ cupping ❏ wear ❏ damage ❏ missing shingles ❏ leaks ❏ exposed nails **Notes:**
			Flashing: ❏ deterioration ❏ loose or detached ❏ bad seals **Notes:**
			Chimney: ❏ loose or crumbling masonry ❏ soot buildup ❏ pests **Notes:**
			Ventilation: ❏ obstructed vents ❏ covers or turbines damaged **Notes:**
			Gutters: ❏ leaks or holes ❏ sags ❏ rust/deterioration ❏ clogs **Notes:**
			Soffits & fascia: ❏ rot ❏ cracks or damage ❏ pests **Notes:**
			Siding & Trim
			Siding: ❏ rot/damage ❏ missing siding ❏ paint failure ❏ buckling **Notes:**
			Trim: ❏ rot/damage ❏ cracks/splits ❏ paint failure **Notes:**
			Doors & Windows
			Weatherstripping: ❏ damaged ❏ missing **Notes:**
			Hardware: ❏ rust/corrosion ❏ paint failure ❏ sticking ❏ misaligned **Notes:**
			Glass & screening: ❏ broken/torn ❏ glazing/retaining strips deteriorated **Notes:**
			Frames, wood: ❏ rot/damage ❏ paint failure **Notes:**
			Foundation
			Leaks: ❏ water in basement ❏ condensation on interior walls **Notes:**
			General condition: ❏ small cracks ❏ large cracks ❏ deterioration **Notes:**
			Decks, Porches & Patios
			Wood surfaces: ❏ rot/damage ❏ paint failure ❏ loose boards **Notes:**
			Masonry surfaces: ❏ cracks ❏ stains ❏ concrete failure **Notes:**
			Railings, trim, accessories: ❏ rust/paint failure ❏ rot/damage **Notes:**
			Driveway & Sidewalks
			Driveway: ❏ cracks ❏ stains ❏ damage **Notes:**
			Sidewalks: ❏ cracks ❏ stains ❏ damage **Notes:**
			Security
			Lighting: ❏ burned-out bulbs ❏ unlit entries **Notes:**
			Locks: ❏ operate smoothly ❏ window locks ❏ strikeplate aligned **Notes:**
			General: ❏ entries unobscured ❏ security system functional **Notes:**

Key: **1**=Good condition **2**=Fair condition: some wear **3**=Needs immediate attention

Comments:

Working Safely

By taking common-sense precautions you can work just as safely outdoors as indoors—even though the exterior presents a few additional safety considerations.

Since many exterior repairs require you to work at heights, learning and following the basic rules of safe ladder and scaffolding use is very important (pages 12 to 13). And any time you are working outside, the weather should play a key role in just about every aspect of how you conduct your work: from the work clothes you select, to the amount of work you decide to undertake.

In addition to the information shown on the following pages, here are some important safety precautions to follow when working outdoors:

• When possible, work with a helper in case there is an emergency. If you have to work alone, inform a friend or family member so they can check on you periodically. If you own a portable telephone, keep it handy at all times.
• Never work at heights, or with tools, if you have consumed alcohol or medication.
• Do not work outdoors in stormy weather. Do not work at heights when it is windy.

Tip for Working Safely

Set up your work site for quick disposal of waste materials. Old nails, jagged metal from flashing, and piles of old shingles all are safety hazards when left on the ground. Use a wheelbarrow to transfer waste to a dumpster or trash can immediately. NOTE: Disposal of building materials is regulated in most areas. Check with your local waste management department.

Wear sensible clothing and protective equipment when working outdoors, including: a cap to protect against direct sunlight, eye protection when working with tools or chemicals, a particle mask when sanding, work gloves, full-length pants, and a long-sleeved shirt. A tool organizer turns a 5-gallon bucket into a safe and convenient container for transporting tools.

Tips for Working Safely

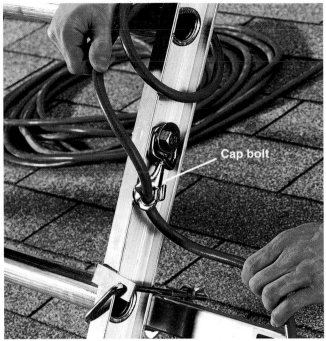

Permanently attach a fastener to the top of your ladder for tying off power cords or air hoses. The weight of a power cord or hose is enough to drag most power tools off the roof. Drill a hole in the ladder and secure a cap bolt (above) to the ladder with a nut and bolt. Do not tie knots in cords and hoses.

Create a storage surface for tools. A sheet of plywood on top of a pair of sawhorses keeps tools off the ground, where they are a safety hazard (and where they can become damaged by moisture). A storage surface also makes it easy to locate tools when you need them.

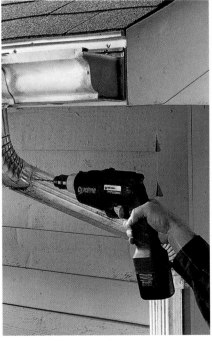

Stay clear of power cables. Household service cables carry 100 amps or electricity or more. If you must work near a cable, use extreme caution, and use fiberglass or wood ladders only—never use metal ladders near cables.

Use a GFCI extension cord when working outdoors. GFCIs (Ground Fault Circuit Interrupters) shut off power if a short circuit occurs (often from contact with water).

Use cordless tools whenever possible to make your work easier and safer. Power cords, even when properly secured, are a nuisance and create many hazards, including tripping and tangling.

Options for Working at Heights

Use an extension ladder for making quick repairs to gutters, fascia, and soffits, and to gain access to roofs. For larger projects, like painting walls, relying solely on ladders is inefficient and dangerous.

Use scaffolding for projects that require you to work at heights for extended periods of time, like preparing walls for paint. If you rent scaffolding, be sure to get assembly-and-use instructions from the rental center.

Tips for Using Ladders and Scaffolds

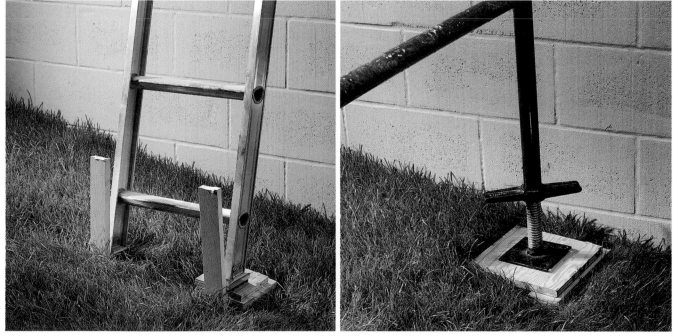

Provide level, stable footing for ladders and scaffolding. Install sturdy blocking under the legs of ladders (left) if the ground is uneven, soft, or slippery, and always drive a stake next to each ladder foot to keep the ladder from slipping away from the house.

Also insert sturdy blocking under scaffold feet (right) if the ground is soft or uneven. Add more blocking under legs in sloped areas, and use the adjustable leg posts for final leveling. If the scaffold has wheels, lock them securely with the hand brakes.

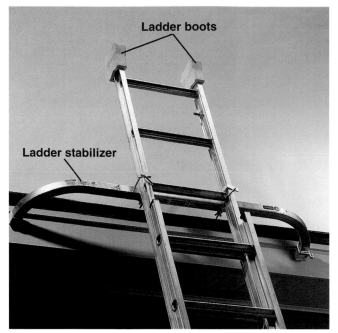

Attach an adjustable ladder stabilizer to your ladder to minimize the chance of slipping. Rest the feet of the stabilizer against broad, flat, stable surfaces only. In addition to making the ladder safer, a stabilizer allows you to work on areas directly in front of the ladder. If you do not use a stabilizer, cover the top ends of the ladder with ladder boots to prevent slipping and protect siding from scratches and dents.

Make sure fly hooks are secure before climbing an extension ladder. The open ends of the hooks should grip a rung on the lower fly extension. Use extra caution when climbing past the fly hooks as you ascend and descend the ladder, and be aware of the points at each fly extension where the doubled rungs end, and single rungs begin.

Anchor ladders and scaffolding by tying them to a secure area, like a chimney—especially if you are not using a ladder stabilizer. If no sturdy anchoring spot exists, create one by driving a #10 screw eye into the fascia. When finished with the ladder, remove the screw eye and cover the hole with caulk.

Ladder Safety Tips:

• Watch out for wires, branches, and overhangs when carrying ladders.

• Position extension ladders so the flat tops of the D-shaped rungs are facing up, parallel to the ground.

• Extend the ladder three feet above the roof edge for greater stability and to provide a gripping point when you mount or dismount the ladder (do not grip too aggressively).

• Do not exceed the work-load rating for your ladder. Limits are listed on the label of any ladder. Read all the safety recommendations.

• Climb on or off a ladder at a point as close to the ground as possible. Move steadily and keep your center of gravity low when crossing between the roof and the ladder.

• Never carry heavy items, like shingle bundles, up an extension ladder. Use a hoist (a simple cord and bucket will do), and pull the items up while you are standing securely on the roof. Lower the items down using the hoist, as well.

Using Caulk & Wood Filler

Caulk is one of the most useful materials for repairing and maintaining your house. It is used to fill gaps, cracks, and holes of every variety. It also is useful as a preventative tool—by sealing exterior seams and gaps with caulk, you keep moisture out of wall cavities and other areas that water can damage. For general exterior purposes, use siliconized acrylic or siliconized latex caulk. These products are flexible, long-lasting, paintable, water resistant, and relatively inexpensive. Use special-purpose caulks, like gutter caulk, when the need arises.

Use two-part epoxy wood fillers to patch or repair wood siding and trim. Do not use standard wood putty; it is not rated for exterior use.

Apply an even bead of caulk by squeezing the release trigger at regular intervals and moving the caulk gun at a steady pace. Practice drawing beads on scraps until you are comfortable with the technique.

Everything You Need:

Tools: caulk gun, utility knife, putty knife, chisel, brush, wooden forms.

Materials: epoxy wood filler, siliconized acrylic caulk, sandpaper, paint, stain.

Choosing Caulk & Wood-repair Products

Epoxy wood filler (A) is an excellent all-purpose product for repairing and patching wood that is exposed to the elements. Most types of epoxy wood filler come with a hardening agent that is mixed in with the product just prior to application. **Wood hardener (B)** is brushed on to damaged or rotted wood to restore strength, often before painting.

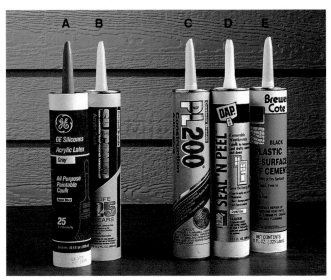

Caulking materials include: tinted exterior caulk to match siding color (A); paintable, siliconized acrylic caulk for general exterior use (B); panel adhesive, for attaching rigid insulation (C); clear, peelable acrylic caulk (D) for weatherstripping around glass; and plastic roof cement (E), for repairing and sealing around shingles, flashing, and miscellaneous areas.

How to Apply Caulk

1 Cut out any old caulk with a utility knife, and clean the surface. Cut the tip of the caulk tube at a 45° angle, using a utility knife or scissors. Puncture the seal at the top of the tube, then load the tube into your caulk gun.

2 Squeeze the trigger of the caulk gun to bring caulk to the tip of the tube, then position the tube at an upper end of the gap being caulked. Draw a continuous bead along the gap. Use caulking backer rope (page 75) for cracks wider than ¼".

3 Finish drawing the bead, then release the plunger in the gun immediately, lifting the gun away from the work area. Failure to release the plunger will cause caulk to continue oozing out of the tube, creating a sticky mess.

How to Repair Wood with Wood Filler

1 Remove all damaged or rotted wood from the repair area, using a wood chisel or a utility knife. Clean away debris with a brush, then wash the repair area. For larger repair areas, attach wood forms to help shape the filler.

2 Prepare the filler for application (see manufacturer's directions), then apply it in the repair area with a putty knife (some fillers may be applied in thick layers, other should not exceed ¼"—read the product directions).

3 After the filler has dried completely, sand with 150-grit sandpaper to shape contours and create a smooth surface. Use a wood file for more extensive shaping. Paint or stain the filler to match the surrounding wood.

Replacing & Repairing Roof Systems

The roof system has a greater exposure to the elements than any other part of your house. As a result, it requires the most attention and the most frequent maintenance. This is especially true because problems in the roof system, like leaks or blocked ventilation, lead quickly to damage in other parts of your house.

A roof system is composed of several elements that work together to provide three basic and essential functions for your home: shelter, drainage, and ventilation. The roof covering and the flashing shed water, directing it to the gutters and downspouts to channel it away from the foundation of your house. Air intake and outtake vents keep fresh air circulating below the roof sheathing, preventing moisture buildup and overheating.

Roof system projects range in complexity, from simply caulking a small hole in a shingle, to removing and replacing shingles, building paper, flashing, and sheathing. Whatever the complex-

ity of the repairs your roof system requires, it is very important that you have a thorough understanding of how all the elements of the system work. By understanding your roof system and making timely repairs, you can ensure that your roof system performs for its full, useful life span.

This sections shows:
- Evaluating Roof Systems (pages 18 to 19)
- Planning a Roofing Project (pages 20 to 21)
- Roofing Materials & Tools (pages 22 to 23)
- Removing Roof Coverings & Replacing Sheathing (pages 24 to 25)
- Installing Drip Edge & Building Paper (pages 26 to 27)
- Installing Flashing (pages 28 to 31)
- Shingling a Roof (pages 32 to 37)
- Repairing Shingles & Flashing (pages 38 to 41)
- Repairing Fascia & Soffits (pages 42 to 45)
- Repairing Gutters (pages 46 to 49)
- Installing a Vinyl Snap-together Gutter System (pages 50 to 51)
- Installing Soffit & Roof Vents (pages 52 to 55)

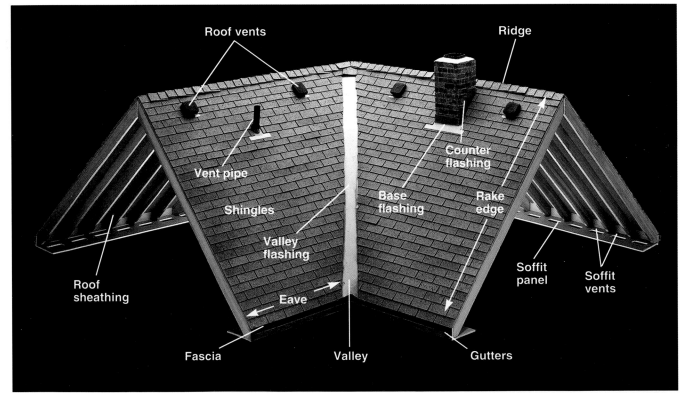

The elements of a roof system work together to provide shelter, drainage, and ventilation. The roof covering is composed of sheathing, building paper, and shingles. Metal flashing is attached in valleys and around chimneys, vent pipes, and other roof elements to seal out water. Soffits cover and protect the eave area below the roof overhang. Fascia, usually attached at the ends of the rafters, supports soffit panels as well as a gutter and downspout system. Soffit vents and roof vents keep fresh air flowing under the roof.

Shown cutaway for clarity

Ice dams occur when melting snow refreezes near the eaves, causing ice to back up under the shingles, where it melts onto the sheathing. To solve the problem, improve roof ventilation (pages 52 to 55).

Evaluating Roof Systems

Regular inspections are essential to maintaining a healthy roof system—more can go wrong in the roof area than in just about any other part of your house. Most roof damage is caused by water, either from precipitation or condensation below the roof materials. Because a failed shingle could be caused by a leak somewhere else in the roof, or by inadequate attic ventilation that results in condensation, simply replacing the shingle will not correct the leak. Make sure you eliminate any moisture source outside the damaged area before you repair the damage.

Finding & Evaluating Roof Leaks

Inspect from inside your attic. Look for discoloration, streaking, or rot on roof sheathing and rafters. Find the highest point of discoloration to pinpoint the source of the leak. Then, measure from the high point to roof vents, chimneys, or other roof elements so you can use their relative locations to help find the leak on the exterior of the roof. If the damage is minimal (left), and no rot has set in, simply repair shingles or flashing (pages 38 to 41). If there is substantial rot (right), tear off the shingles above the rot, replace damaged sheathing (page 25), and reshingle (pages 26 to 36). Fix any moisture problems outside the damaged area.

Common Shingle Problems

Buckled shingles (top) and **cupped shingles** (bottom) usually are caused by lingering moisture beneath the shingle. Likely sources include condensation from poor attic ventilation (pages 52 to 55), or leaky shingles or flashing. If you find and fix the moisture problem, buckled shingles may flatten out by themselves. If they do not flatten out, replace them. Cupped shingles almost always require replacement. See pages 24 to 36 for major damage, or pages 38 to 39 for isolated damage. Do not install new shingles over cupped or buckled shingles.

Damaged shingles (top) and **worn shingles** (bottom) become increasingly common as a roof ages. Damage can occur on any roof, new or old, but it becomes more likely as the shingles age and the protective mineral surfaces wear down. Treat isolated damage or wear by replacing only the problem shingles (pages 38 to 41). Widespread damage and pervasive wear usually require that all the shingles be replaced, either by tearing off and reshingling (pages 24 to 36), or by installing new shingles over the old shingles (page 37—check building codes first).

Gutter Problems

Sagging gutters can be caused by deteriorated fascia or by weight from a blockage. Remove the blockage (page 117), replace damaged fascia (page 43), then raise and refasten gutters (page 46).

Leaking gutters usually result from holes or separated joints (shown). Disassemble leaky joints, then caulk and reassemble the joint (page 48). Patch holes (pages 47 to 48).

Damaged gutter sections should be patched (pages 47 to 48) or replaced (page 49). If damage is widespread, replace with a new gutter system (pages 50 to 51).

Flashing Problems

Loose flashing can be caused by external forces, like high wind, or by failure of sealant or fasteners. To repair, pull back the flashing enough to clean out the old sealant, and resecure with fresh roofing cement and new fasteners (page 38).

Damaged and deteriorated flashing are primary causes of roof leaks. Remove and replace the damaged piece (page 40). If several pieces are damaged or showing signs of wear, remove and replace all the flashing around the affected roof element (page 41).

Fascia & Soffit Problems

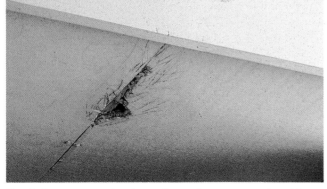

Pest damage and rot are the primary enemies of soffits. Small spots of damage can be repaired by replacing the material (pages 44 to 45). If damage is more widespread, or if your house does not have soffits, and birds or insects are nesting in your eaves, install a new soffit system (page 42).

Rotten fascia is easy to spot from the ground on homes with no gutter system. If your house has gutters, climb up and check for rot behind the gutters, especially if they are sagging. Replace damaged sections of fascia (page 43), removing the gutters where necessary.

Planning a Roofing Project

Planning makes any project go more smoothly, and working on your roof is no exception.

Measure the square footage of your roof so you can estimate materials and time. When estimating materials, add 15% to allow for waste. Shop around to compare shingle prices, then make a rough cost estimate for the type you select. Count the number of roof elements, like vent pipes, vent fans, skylights, dormers, and chimneys, that you will need to roof around, and tally up the costs for the flashing needed for these elements. Check your sheathing from the attic side. If replacement is needed, make a cost allowance for it. Add in additional materials costs, like building paper, roof cement, nails, dumpster rental, and tool purchase or rental.

Next, estimate the time your project will demand (see chart, next page). Calculate the slope of the roof so you can determine if you need roof jacks to move around. If so, take that into account when making time estimates. By making reasonable estimates, you can divide the project into manageable portions.

Most building centers will deliver shingles, building paper, and other materials directly to your roof, using a mechanical lift. If you can arrange it, have at least one section of the old roof torn off, with new building paper and drip edge installed, before shingle delivery. This will save time, as well as energy you would use to hoist the heavy shingle bundles up from the ground and reposition them on your roof.

Dress for protection and safety when working on roof projects. Wear rubber-soled shoes for good traction, knee pads, a nail apron, a tool belt, a long-sleeved shirt, full-length pants, and work gloves. Always wear protective eyewear when nailing or using power tools.

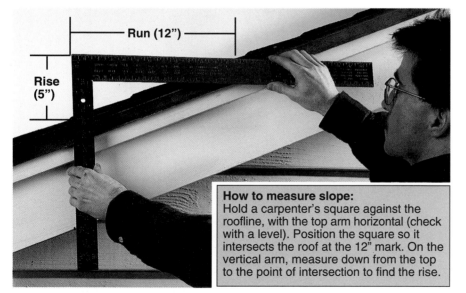

> **How to measure slope:**
> Hold a carpenter's square against the roofline, with the top arm horizontal (check with a level). Position the square so it intersects the roof at the 12" mark. On the vertical arm, measure down from the top to the point of intersection to find the rise.

Calculate the slope of your roof before beginning any roofing project. Slope is usually described by the number of inches the roof rises in each foot along a horizontal plane (called the "run"). For example, the roof shown above has a 5-in-12 slope: it rises 5" in 12" of run. Knowing the slope is important for selecting materials, and to help gauge the difficulty of moving on the roof. Use roof jacks if the slope is 7-in-12 or steeper. Roofs with a slope of 3-in-12 or less must have a fully bonded covering.

Tips for Planning a Roofing Project

Estimating time requirements			
Task	**Time Requirement**	**Amount**	**Total Time**
Tear-off	1 hr./square*		•
Install building paper	30 min./square		•
Apply shingles:			
Flat run	2 hrs./square		•
Ridges, hips	30 min./10 ft		•
Dormers**	add 1 hr. ea.		•
•Flashing:			
Chimneys	2 hrs. ea.		•
Vent pipes	30 min. ea.		•
Valleys	30 min./10 ft.		•
Roof vents	30 min. ea.		•
Skylights	2 hrs. ea.		•
Drip edge	30 min./20 ft.		•
TOTAL TIME FOR PROJECT			•

NOTE: All time estimates are based on one worker. Reduce time by 40% if there is a helper.
*One square=100 square feet
**Include area of dormer surface in "flat run" estimate

Protect against damage from falling materials when tearing off old shingles. Hang tarps over the sides of the house, and lean plywood against the house to protect vegetation.

How to Install Roof Jacks

"Dead area"

1 Nail roof jacks to the roof at the fourth or fifth course. Position the jacks so the nail slots are in the "dead area" where shingles will not be exposed, then drive a 16d nail into each slot. Install one jack every 4 ft., with 6" to 12" of overhang at the ends of the board.

2 Shingle over the tops of the roof jacks (when installing shingles), then rest a 2 × 8 or 2 × 10 board on the support arms of the jacks—use the widest board the supports will hold. Drive a nail through the hole in the lip of each roof jack to secure the board.

Tip of pry bar over nail heads

3 Remove boards and roof jacks when the project is complete. Drive in 16d nails by positioning the end of a pry bar over each nail head, then rapping the shank of the pry bar with a hammer.

Choose a roof covering that is a good match for your house and your budget. *Asphalt or fiberglass shingles* (left) are by far the most popular choice because they are relatively inexpensive, durable, easy to install, and available in a wide variety of styles and colors. Look for shingles with a 20-year warranty. *Wood shakes* (center) are usually made from natural split cedar. They are more expensive and more time-consuming to install than shingles. *Clay tiles* (right) create a very distinctive appearance, but they are fairly expensive and should only be installed by a professional.

Roofing Materials & Tools

Most do-it-yourselfers select asphalt or fiberglass shingles because they are inexpensive and simple to install. The most common type are "3-tab" shingles, which contain three 12"-wide tabs, separated by slots. Less common coverings, like cedar shakes and clay tiles, are best installed by a professional, but you can save money by doing the tear-off and preparation work yourself. If your roof has a slope of 3-in-12 (page 20) or less, you need a "fully-bonded" roof covering, usually made of built-up tar or sheets of roll roofing that are bonded to the sheathing with roof cement (also a good job for a professional).

How to estimate shingles:
Shingles are sold in bundles, but estimated in *squares*—the amount needed to cover 100 square feet. Three bundles of shingles cover one square. To estimate how many bundles you need, calculate the square footage of roof area, and add 15% for waste. Divide the total by 100, then multiply by 3 to find the number of bundles needed for your project.

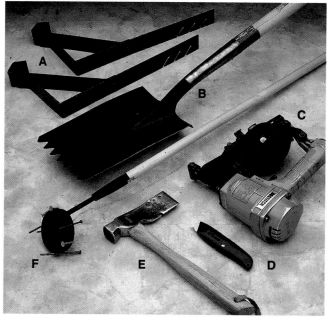

Specialty roofing tools include: roof jacks (A), roofing shovel with slots in the blade for tearing off shingles and prying out nails (B), pneumatic nailer (C), utility knife with hook blade (D), roofing hammer with alignment guides and hatchet-style blade (E), and a release magnet for site cleanup (F).

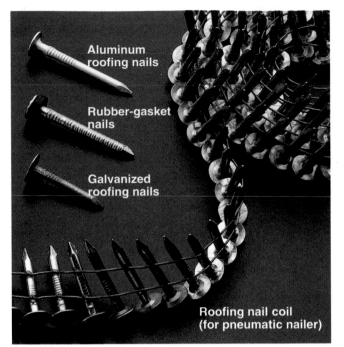

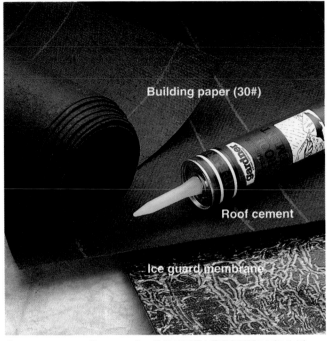

Use the right fastener for the job. Use galvanized roofing nails to hand-nail shingles (buy two pounds of nails per square of shingles); use aluminum nails for aluminum flashing, and rubber-gasket nails for galvanized metal flashing. Use roofing nail coils for pneumatic nailers (check coverage chart on carton).

Common roofing materials include: 30# building paper for shingle underlayment; cartridges of plastic roofing cement; and ice-guard membrane for use as underlayment in the first course or two of roofs in cold climates (page 26).

Roof flashing can be hand-cut or purchased in pre-formed shapes and sizes. Cut rolled flashing material with aviator snips to make longer flashing pieces, like valley flashing (also available pre-formed), or non-standard pieces, like base flashing and top saddles (pages 30 to 31). Most experienced roofers buy step flashing blanks in standard sizes, and bend them to fit their project. Drip edge and vent pipe flashing should be purchased as pre-formed pieces. Skylights usually are sold complete with a flashing kit. Complicated flashing pieces, like chimney crickets (page 31), should be made by a professional metalworker.

Cover unshingled sections overnight, using tarps weighted down with shingle bundles. Tear off only one roof section at a time if you cannot reshingle the entire roof in one day.

Removing Roof Coverings & Replacing Sheathing

Completely remove old shingles, building paper, and flashing if your old roof already has more than one layer of shingles; if shingles are cupped or buckled; or if sheathing is damaged. Replace damaged sheathing after the roof covering is off.

Rent a dumpster from a waste disposal company or your local waste management department, and position it below the roof edge for direct dumping of materials. Or, arrange wheelbarrows on tarps to catch debris. Use extreme caution during tear-off: debris on the roof is a serious hazard.

Everything You Need:

Tools: dumpster, hammer, chisel, pry bar, roofing knife, roofing shovel, broom, release magnet, rake, tin snips, reciprocating saw, drill.

Materials: protective gear, tarps, plywood sheets, 2 × 4 nailing strips, sheathing material, galvanized deck screws.

How to Tear Off Old Roof Coverings

1 Slice through roofing cement around flashing to release it from the shingles. Remove any flashing that you plan to replace. NOTE: Unless the flashing is in exceptional condition, it is easier to remove and replace all the flashing during a full shingle tear-off. Save complicated flashing pieces, like chimney saddles or crickets, and reuse, if practical.

2 Remove the ridge cap, using a pry bar. With the ridge cap out of the way, start prying up the top course of shingles with a roofing shovel or flat pry bar. Work on only one roof section at a time.

3 Remove old shingles and building paper in large sections, using a roofing shovel. Work from top to bottom. NOTE: The tear-off portion of a roofing project is an ideal time to get help. Having another person to dispose of the materials before they can accumulate on the ground is a great time-saver. Make sure your helper is out of the way before you dump materials.

4 After removing shingles and building paper from the entire tear-off section, pry out any remaining nails. Also sweep the roof with a garage broom to prepare it for the building paper. TIP: Clean up nails on the ground with a release magnet (page 22).

How to Replace Damaged Sheathing

1 Cut out damaged sheathing boards with a reciprocating saw (check inside for wiring first). Cut next to rafters in an area that extends well beyond the damaged material. Pry out the damaged sections.

2 Attach 2 x 4 nailing strips to the rafters at the edges of the cutout sections Using 3" deck screws.

3 Cut sheathing patches from exterior-grade plywood the same thickness as the old sheathing, allowing for a ⅛"-wide expansion gap on all sides. Attach the patch with 2¼" deck screws or 8d ring-shank siding nails, driven into rafters and nailing strips.

Installing Drip Edge & Building Paper

Drip edge is flashing that is installed at the edges of your roof to direct water flow away from the roof sheathing. Building paper is installed on roof decks as insurance in case leaks develop in shingles or flashing. It is sold in several weights, but 30# paper is a good choice for use under shingles (15# meets code in some areas). Check with your local building inspector.

In colder climates, recent changes to building codes require a special type of underlayment, called "ice guard" or "ice shield," instead of standard building paper for the first course or two of underlayment. An adhesive membrane, the ice guard bonds with the sheathing to create a barrier to runoff from ice dams (page 18).

Work your way up the roof deck with building paper courses, allowing 4" horizontal overlaps and 12" vertical seams. Roll building paper across valleys from both sides (photo, above), overlapping the ends by 36". Overlap hips and ridges by 6". Attach building paper with a hammer stapler, driving a staple every 6" to 12" at the edges, and one staple per square foot in the field area.

> **Everything You Need:**
>
> Tools: hammer, pry bar, roofing knife, hammer stapler, chalk line, tape measure, tin snips.
>
> Materials: drip edge, 30# building paper, roofing cement, ice guard, roofing nails.

Tips for Installing Drip Edge

Eave edge

Rake edge

Attach at eaves _before_ attaching building paper.
Nail a strip of drip edge along the edge of the eaves. Overlap strips by 2" at vertical seams. Miter the ends at a 45° angle to make a miter joint with the drip edge on the rake edge. Install galvanized and vinyl drip edge with galvanized roofing nails. Use aluminum nails for aluminum drip edge. Nail at 12" intervals.

Attach at rake edges _after_ attaching building paper.
Start at the bottom, forming a miter joint with the drip edge at the eaves. Work toward the ridge, overlapping pieces of drip edge by 2" (make sure the higher strip is on top at overlaps).

Tips for Installing Building Paper & Ice Guard Underlayment

Snap a chalk line 35⅝" up from the eave edge, so the first course of the 36"-wide ice guard membrane (or building paper) overhangs the eaves by ⅜". Install a course of ice guard, using the chalk line as a reference. Peel back the protective backing as you unroll the ice guard. In cold climates, apply as many courses of ice guard as it takes to cover 24" past the roof overhang. In warm climates, ice guard may not be necessary, so check your local codes.

Measure up from the eave edge to a point 32" above the top of the previous course of underlayment, and snap another chalk line. Roll out the next course of building paper (or ice guard, if required), overlapping the first course by 4". Install building paper up to the ridge, ruled side up, snapping horizontal lines every two or three rows to check alignment. Always overlap from above. Trim off courses flush with the rake edge.

Fit a building paper patch over any obstructions, like vent pipes or roof vents. Apply building paper up to the obstruction, then resume laying the course on the opposite side (make sure to maintain the line). Cut a patch that overlaps the building paper by 12" on all sides. Make a cross-hatch cutout for the obstruction. Position the patch, staple in place, then caulk seams with roof cement.

Tuck building paper under siding at the bottoms of dormers and sidewalls, where they intersect with the roof. Also tuck it under counterflashing on chimneys (page 31) and skylights. Carefully pry up the siding, and tuck at least 2" of paper under the siding. Do not refasten siding or counterflashing right away—wait until after you install step flashing (page 30).

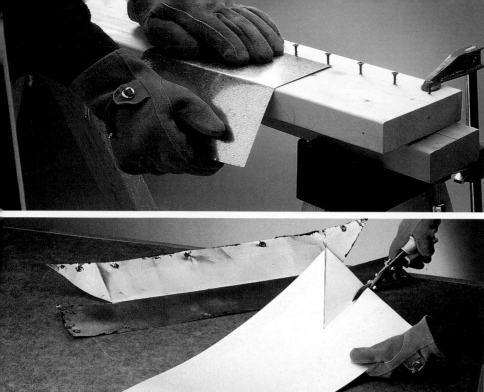

Installing Flashing

Flashing is a metal or rubber barrier used to protect the seams around roof elements. Many beginning roofers consider flashing installation to be the most difficult element of a roofing project. But once you learn one or two basic principles of installing flashing, the mystery disappears quickly.

The purpose of flashing is to make water flow over shingled surfaces, and away from gaps around roof elements, like vent pipes and chimneys. To accomplish this, pieces of flashing are layered between rows of shingles.

Around roof elements, flashing should be secured to one surface only—usually the roof deck. Use only roof cement to bond the flashing to the roof elements. Flashing must be able to flex as the roof element and the roof deck expand and contract (usually at different rates). If flashing is fastened to both the roof deck and the roof element, it will tear or loosen.

NOTE: In this section, we show you how to install flashing during a shingle-installation project (pages 32 to 36). For information on repairing or replacing flashing, see pages 38 to 41. Also see page 23 for flashing product information.

Bend your own flashing (top). Make a bending jig by driving screws into a piece of scrap wood, creating a line one-half the width of the flashing when measured from the edge of the board. Clamp the bending jig to a worksurface, then press a step flashing blank (page 23) flat on the board. Bend it over the edge. **Use old flashing as a template** (bottom) for making replacement flashing. This is especially useful for reproducing complicated flashing, like saddle flashing for chimneys or dormers.

Tip for Installing Flashing

Replace flashing during shingle installation. Because most roof flashing is interwoven with shingles, you will get better results than if you try to retrofit flashing around existing shingles.

Everything You Need:

Tools: tape measure, roofing hammer, pry bar, trowel, caulk gun, aviator snips.

Materials: roof cement, roofing nails, rubber gasket nails, galvanized metal flashing, vent pipe flashing, shingles.

How to Install Metal Valley Flashing

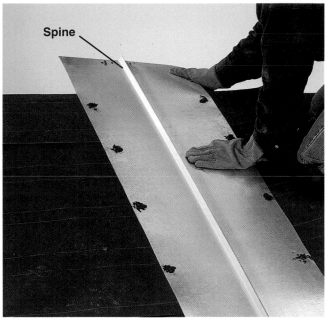

1 After installing building paper across the valley (page 26), set a piece of valley flashing (preformed or bent from rolled flashing) into the valley, so the bottom of the "V" rests in the crease of the valley. Starting at the eave, nail the flashing near each edge at 12" intervals. Trim the end of the flashing at the eave so it is flush with the drip edges at each side. Add pieces, moving up toward the ridge. Overlap from above by at least 8".

2 Add overlapping pieces, working toward the ridge, until the flashing reaches a few inches past the ridge. Bend the flashing over the ridge, so it lies flat on the opposite side of the roof. If you are installing preformed flashing, make a small cut in the spine for easier bending. Cover nail heads with roof cement (unless you used rubber-gasket nails). Also apply roof cement at the side edges of the flashing.

How to Install Vent Pipe Flashing

1 Shingle up to the vent pipe. Cut the top shingle to fit around the pipe, so the "reveal area" of the shingle (the exposed portion) is within 5" of the pipe. Apply roof cement to the base of the flashing.

2 Slip the sleeve of the flashing over the vent pipe, making sure the pitch of the flange is sloped in the right direction. Press the flange against the roof deck, then fasten with rubber-gasket nails.

3 Continue installing shingle courses, making cutouts for the pipe. Do not nail through the flashing—attach shingles with roof cement where they cover flashing.

How to Install Step Flashing

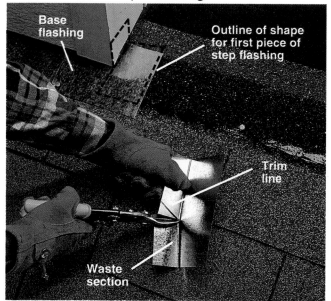

1 Shingle up to the element requiring flashing (here, a dormer) so the tops of the reveal areas are within 5" of the element. Install base flashing (step 1, next page). Bend a piece of step flashing in half, and set the piece next to the lowest corner of the element. Mark a trim line on the flashing, following the vertical edge of the element. Cut off the waste part of the flashing (the area ouside the trim line on the vertical side of the bend), making a starter cut first.

2 Pry out the lower courses of siding and any trim at the base of the element. Insert spacers to prop trim or siding away from the work area. Apply roof cement to the base flashing in the area where the overlap with the step flashing will be formed. Tuck the trimmed piece of step flashing under the propped area, and press the flashing into the roof cement. Fasten the flashing with one rubber-gasket nail driven near the top, and into the roof deck.

3 Apply roof cement to the top side of the first piece of step flashing, where it will be covered by the next shingle course. Install the shingle, setting it firmly into the roof cement. Do not nail through the flashing when attaching shingles. Apply roof cement to the shingle, next to the dormer or other roof element (in the area that will be covered by the next piece of step flashing).

4 Tuck another piece of step flashing under the trim or siding, setting it into the roof cement on the shingle. Overlap the first piece of step flashing by at least 2". Continue flashing in this manner until you reach the top of the element. Trim the last piece of flashing to fit at the top corner of the element. Refasten siding and trim. On chimneys or other elements needing a top saddle (step 3, next page), the saddle should overlap the last piece of step flashing.

How to Install Chimney Flashing

1 Shingle up to the chimney base. Cut base flashing, using the old base flashing as a template (page 28). Bend up counterflashing (the flashing anchored in the chimney to cover the step flashing). Apply roof cement to the base of the chimney and the shingles just below the base. Press the base flashing into the roof cement, and bend the flashing around the edges of the chimney. Drive rubber-gasket nails through the flashing flange and into the roof deck.

2 Apply step flashing and shingles (previous page), working up toward the top of the chimney. Fasten the flashing to the chimney with roof cement only, and fold down counterflashing as you go.

3 Cut and install top flashing (sometimes called a saddle) around the high side of the chimney, overlapping the final piece of step flashing along each side. Attach with roof cement on both the roof deck and the chimney, and rubber-gasket nails driven through the base of the flashing and into the roof deck. Continue shingling past the chimney, using roof cement (not nails) to attach shingles over flashing.

TIP: If your roof originally had a cricket to divert water around the chimney, have a new cricket made by a metalworker. Provide the fabricator with either the old cricket to use as a template, or the roof slope (page 20) and the chimney width to use as a guide. Secure the cricket in place with roof cement on all flanges, and drive rubber-gasket nails through the base flanges and into the roof deck. Bend counterflashing back down, and fill the gap with roof cement.

Shingling a Roof

If you have the time and the energy, shingling a roof can be a straightforward project that is well within the abilities of most do-it-yourselfers. The most common type of shingles, asphalt 3-tabs, are self-sealing and self-aligning. Installation is mainly a matter of persistence and making sure you follow your lines and shingle pattern.

Because most roof flashing is interwoven into the shingle pattern, be prepared to install all your flashing (pages 28 to 31) during the shingling process. Install building paper and drip edge before you start (pages 26 to 27).

Everything You Need:

Tools: tape measure, roofing hammer, pneumatic nailer (optional), pry bar, roofing knife, chalk line, carpenter's square, straightedge, roof jacks and 2 × 10 lumber, aviator snips.

Materials: roofing nails, nailing cartridges (optional), roof cement, flashing, shingles.

Stagger shingles for effective protection against leaks. If the tab slots are aligned in successive rows, water forms channels, increasing erosion of the mineral surface of the shingles. Creating a 6" offset between rows of shingles (with the 3-tab shingles shown above) ensures that the tab slots do not align.

How to Shingle a Roof with 3-tab Shingles

1 Snap a chalk line onto the first course of ice guard or building paper, 11½" up from the eave edge, to create an alignment line for the starter course of shingles. This will result in a ½" shingle overhang past the edge of the roof for standard 12" shingles. TIP: Do not use red chalk—it will stain roofing materials.

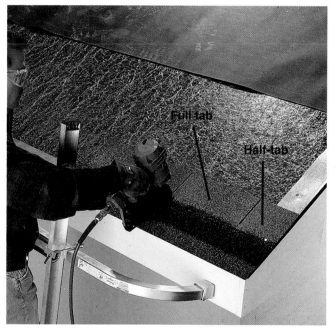

2 Install the starter row: Trim off one-half (6") of an end tab on one shingle. Position the shingle so the tabs are aligned with the chalk line, with the half-tab flush against the rake edge. Drive ⅞" roofing nails near each end, and about 1" down from each slot between tabs. Butt a full shingle next to the trimmed shingle, and nail in place. Fill out the row, trimming the last shingle flush with the opposite rake edge.

3 Apply the first full course of shingles over the starter course, with the tabs pointing down. Begin at the rake edge where you began the starter row. The first shingle should overhang the rake edge by ⅜", and overhang the eave edge by ½". Make sure the tops of the shingles are flush with the tops of the shingles in the starter course, following the chalk line.

4 Snap a chalk line from the eave edge to the ridge to create a vertical shingle alignment line. Choose an area with no obstructions, as close as possible to the center of the roof. The chalk line should pass through a slot or a shingle edge on the first full shingle course. Use a carpenter's square to establish a line that is perpendicular with the eave edge.

NOTE: Do not nail shingles in spots where they do not overlap another shingle. Upper-course shingles must be pulled back to fill in lower courses.

Vertical line

18"
12"
6"
5" reveal

5 Use the vertical line to establish a shingle pattern with slots that are offset by 6" in succeeding courses. Tack down a shingle 6" to one side of the vertical line to start the second course. The bottom of the shingle should be 5" above the bottoms of the first-course shingles. Tack down shingles for the third and fourth courses 12" and 18" away from the vertical line. Start the fifth course against the vertical line.

6 Fill in shingles in the second through fifth courses, working upward from the second course and maintaining a consistent 5" reveal. Slide lower-course shingles under any upper-course shingles left partially nailed, then nail down. NOTE: Install roof jacks, if needed, after filling out the fifth course (page 21).

(continued next page)

TIP: Check the alignment of your shingles after each four-course cycle. In several spots on the top course, measure from the bottom edges of the shingles to the nearest building-paper line. If you discover any misalignment, distribute adjustments over the next few rows until the misalignment is corrected.

7 When you reach obstructions, like dormers, shingle a full course above them so you can retain your shingle offset pattern. On the unshingled side of the obstruction, snap another vertical reference line, using the shingles above the obstruction as a guide.

8 Shingle upward from the eave on the other side of the obstruction, using the vertical line as a reference for reestablishing your shingle slot offset pattern. Fill out the shingle courses past the rake edges of the roof, then trim off the excess (step 15).

9 Trim off some of the excess shingle material at the the "V"s in valley flashing wherever two roof decks join (these edges will be trimmed back farther at a slight taper after both roof decks are shingled). Do not cut into flashing.

10 Install shingles on adjoining roof decks, starting at the bottom edge, using the same offset alignment pattern used on the other roof decks (steps 1 to 6). Install shingles until courses overlap the center of the valley flashing at the joint between roof decks. Trim shingles at both sides of the valley when finished (step 14).

11 When you reach a hip (any peak where two sections of roof meet) or the ridge (the hip at the top of your roof), shingle up the first roof side until the tops of the uppermost reveal areas are within 5" of the hip or ridge. Trim the excess off along the joint at the peak. Overlap the ridge or hip (no more than 5") with the top shingle course on the other side of the peak.

TIP: Cut three 12"-square ridge/hip caps from each 3-tab shingle. With the top surface facing down, cut the shingles at the tab lines, trimming off both top corners of the 12"-square cap shingles (trimming corners prevents unsightly overlaps in the reveal area).

12 Snap a chalk line 6" down from the hip or ridge on one side, parallel to the peak. Begin attaching cap shingles at one end, aligned with the chalk line. Drive two 1¼" roofing nails per cap, about 1" in from each edge, just below the seal strip.

(continued next page)

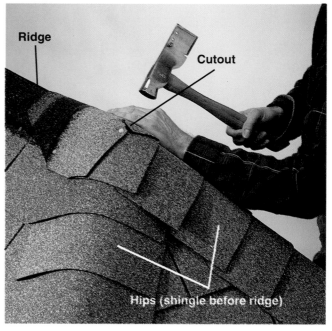

13 Install cap shingles halfway along the ridge or hip, creating a 5" reveal for each cap. Follow the chalk line. Then, starting at the opposite end of the ridge or hip, install caps over the other half of the roof. Cut a 5"-wide section from the reveal area of a shingle tab, and use it as a "closure cap" to cover the joint where the caps meet.

VARIATION: Wherever roof hips join with roof ridges, shingle to the top of each hip with cap shingles. Then, make a cutout in the center of a ridge cap, set the cap at the end of the ridge, and bend the corners so they fit over the hips. Secure each corner with a roofing nail, and cover nail heads with roof cement.

14 After all shingles are installed, trim the shingles at the valleys to create a gap that is 3" wide at the ridge, and widens at a rate of ⅛" per foot toward the eave edge. Use a utility knife with a roofing blade and a straightedge (be careful not to cut through the valley flashing). At the valleys, seal the undersides and edges of the shingles with roof cement. Also cover any exposed nail heads with roof cement.

15 Trim the shingles at the rake edges of the roof, using a utility knife with a hooked roofing blade (or you can use aviator snips). Leave a ⅜" overhang. Always use a straightedge to ensure a straight cut.

Variation: How to Shingle Over an Old Roof

Trim new shingles to fit

1 Cut tabs off shingles and install the remaining strips over the reveal area of the old first course, creating a flat surface for the starter row of new shingles. Use 1¼"-long roofing nails. NOTE: Read the section on shingling a roof (pages 32 to 36) before you start.

2 Trim the tops off shingles for the first course. The shingles should be sized to butt against the bottom edges of the old third course, overhanging the roof edge by ½". Install the shingles so the tab slots do not align with the slots in the old shingles.

Cutout in old shingles to create a flat surface for the base flange of vent pipe flashing

3 Using the old shingles to direct your layout, begin installing the new shingles. Maintain a consistent tab slot offset (page 33, step 5). Shingle up toward the roof ridge, stopping before the final course. Install flashing as you proceed (see next step). If valley flashing is in good condition, it does not need to be replaced.

4 Replace old flashing during the shingling sequence (pages 28 to 31). A "roofover" is flashed using the same techniques and materials used for shingling over building paper, except you need to trim or fill in shingles around vent pipes and roof vents to create a flat surface for the base flange of the flashing pieces.

5 Tear off old hip and ridge caps before shingling the hips and ridge. Replace old hip and ridge caps after all other shingling is completed (pages 35 to 36).

Repairing Shingles & Flashing

Roof materials that have sustained minimal damage or wear can be patched or repaired, avoiding the expense and work of replacing some or all of your roof. Plastic roof cement and rolled, galvanized flashing can be used for many simple roof repairs. TIP: Heat brittle shingles with a hair dryer to make them easier to handle.

Everything You Need:

Tools: hammer, pry bar, caulk gun, utility knife with roofing blade, pointed trowel, hacksaw, rubber mallet.

Materials: flashing, roof coverings, roof cement, roofing nails, 30# building paper.

Use plastic roof cement for a variety of minor repairs, like reattaching loose shingles. Wipe down the building paper and the underside of the shingle, let them dry, then apply roof cement liberally. Seat the shingle in the bed of cement.

Tips for Making Repairs with Roof Cement

Tack down buckled shingles by cleaning out below the buckled area, filling with roof cement, and pressing the shingle in the cement. Also use roof cement to patch cracks or other minor shingle problems. See page 18 for more information on buckled shingles.

Seal gaps around flashing by cleaning out the old roof cement and replacing it with fresh roof cement. Joints around flashing are common places for roof leaks to occur.

How to Replace a Section of Shingles

1 Pull out damaged shingles in the repair area, beginning with the uppermost shingle. Be careful not to damage any surrounding shingles that are in good condition.

2 Remove old nails with a flat pry bar. Exposed nail heads will cause punctures in new shingles. Important: remove nails in the shingle above the repair area to enable you to nail new shingles. Cover holes or damage in the building paper with roof cement.

3 Install replacement shingles, beginning with the lowest shingle in the repair area. Nail above tab slots with ⅞" or 1" roofing nails. TIP: Asphalt shingles can be aged to match surrounding shingles by wiping the surface with mineral spirits. Rinse before installing.

Seal line

4 Install all but the top shingle with nails (pages 32 to 33), then apply roof cement to the underside of the top shingle, above the seal line.

5 Slip last shingle into place under the overlapping shingle. Press the shingle into the roof cement. Lift up the shingle above the repair area, and nail the top replacement shingle in place.

How to Replace Wood Shakes & Shingles

1 Split the damaged shake (shown) or shingle, using a hammer and chisel, and remove the pieces. Pry out (cut nails in overlapping shingles with a hacksaw blade slipped underneath the shingle).

2 Gently pry up shingles or shakes above the repair area. Cut new shingles or shakes for the lowest course, leaving about ⅜" for expansion. Nail replacement pieces in place with ring-shank siding nails. Fill in all but the top course.

3 Cut pieces for the top course, slip them beneath the overlapping shingles, and face-nail them in place near the tops. Cover all exposed nail heads with roof cement, then wipe off the excess. TIP: Apply wood sealer or stain to "weather" new material.

How to Patch Damaged Flashing

1 Measure the damaged area and cut a patch from flashing material of the same type as the original flashing. The patch should be wide enough to slip under the shingles at each side of the repair area. Break the seal between the valley flashing and the shingles around the damaged area. Scrub the damaged flashing with a wire brush, and wipe clean.

2 Apply a bed of roof cement to the back side of the patch, then slip the patch under the shingles on each side of the repair area. Press the patch securely into the roof cement. Add cement at the seams and the shingle joints. Feather out the cement to prevent damming of water. NOTE: New flashing material will blend in quickly as natural forces cause the metal to discolor.

How to Replace Step Flashing

1 Carefully bend up counterflashing (or pry out siding) covering the damaged step flashing. Cut roof cement seals, and pull back the shingles covering damaged step flashing. Remove the damaged piece or pieces of flashing with a flat pry bar.

2 Cut new step flashing from the same type of metal (aluminum or galvanized steel) used for the old flashing. Apply roof cement to the flashing on both unexposed sides. Slip the flashing into place, making sure it is overlapped by the flashing above it, and that it overlaps the flashing below. It also must overlap the shingle beneath it. Drive one roofing nail through the flashing at the bottom corner, and into the roof deck. Do not fasten to the roof element.

3 Bend counterflashing back down, and seal the counterflashing seams with roof cement.

4 Lift shingles next to the repair area, then apply fresh roof cement to the undersides and to any exposed nail heads. Press the shingles down against the flashing to create a bond. Do not nail flashing when attaching shingles.

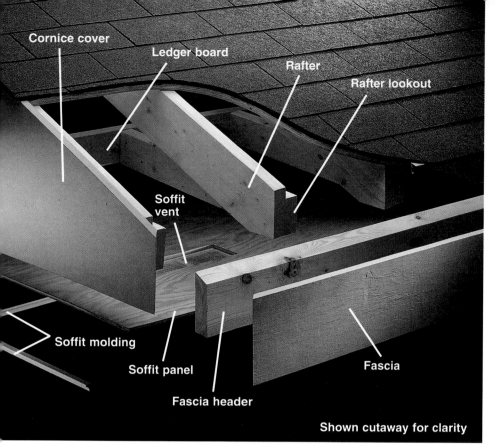

Cornice cover
Ledger board
Rafter
Rafter lookout
Soffit vent
Soffit molding
Soffit panel
Fascia header
Fascia

Shown cutaway for clarity

Fascia and soffits close off the eave area beneath the roof overhang. The fascia covers the ends of rafters and rafter lookouts, and provides a surface for attaching gutters. Soffits are protective panels that span the area between the fascia and the side of the house. Some soffit types attach to fascia headers (above), while others fit into grooves cut in the back sides of the fascia. Soffit moldings and ledger boards are used to mount the soffit panels at the side of the house.

Option: Install a New Soffit System

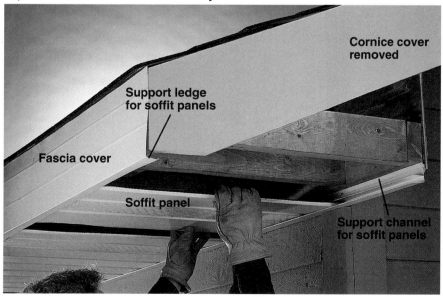

Cornice cover removed
Support ledge for soffit panels
Fascia cover
Soffit panel
Support channel for soffit panels

Install a new soffit system if your old system has failed, or pests have infested the open eave areas of your roof overhang. A complete soffit system consists of fabricated fascia covers, soffit panels (nonventilated or ventilated), and support channels that hold the panels at the sides of your house. Most soffit systems sold at building centers are made of aluminum or vinyl. Follow manufacturer's instructions for installation.

Repairing Fascia & Soffits

Fascia and soffits add a finished look to your roof, and promote a healthy roof system. A well-ventilated fascia/soffit system prevents moisture from building up under the roof and in the attic. A secure system keeps pests, like birds and bats, from nesting in the eaves.

Usually fashioned from dimension lumber, fascia is attached to rafters or rafter lookouts (photo, left). While enhancing the appearance of your home, it also provides a stable surface for hanging gutters.

Repairing fascia and soffits is easy. Most problems can be corrected by cutting out the damaged material and replacing it with new material. Joints between fascia boards are lock-nailed (page 43), so you should remove whole sections of fascia to make accurate miter cuts for patches. Soffits usually are not removed for repairs (pages 44 to 45).

Fasten soffit and fascia material with ring-shank siding nails, or use galvanized deck screws. Nails are easier to work with in some cases, but screws provide more holding power.

Whenever repairing soffits, take a moment to inspect vents in the system for sufficient air flow (pages 52 to 54).

Everything You Need:

Tools: circular saw, jig saw, drill, hammer, flat pry bar, chisel, nail set.

Materials: replacement materials to match damaged parts, nailing strips, nails or screws, caulk, primer, paint.

How to Repair Fascia

1 Remove gutters, shingle moldings, and any other material that prevents removal of the damaged section of fascia.

2 Using a flat pry bar, remove the entire damaged section all the way to the next fascia board. Remove old nails.

3 Cut off the damaged portion of the fascia board. Set your circular saw to make a miter cut, and saw at a rafter location (look for nail holes to identify the rafter location).

4 Attach the undamaged original fascia, using 2" galvanized deck screws driven into rafter lookouts or rafters. Cut a patch board with a matching miter at the mating end to replace the damaged section.

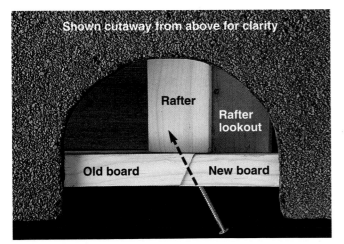

5 Attach the patch board. Drill pilot holes, then drive nails at an angle through the mitered ends of both boards, creating a lock-nail joint.

6 Reattach the shingle moldings and trim, using 4d galvanized finish nails. Set nail heads. Prime and paint the patch to match the fascia. Reattach gutters.

How to Repair Wood-panel Soffits

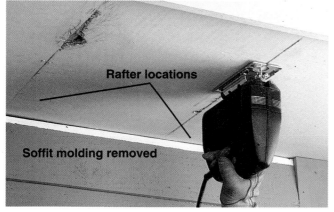

Rafter locations

Soffit molding removed

1 Remove the support molding in the damaged area. Drill entry holes for a jig saw blade, then cut out the soffit area that contains the damage. Saw as close as possible to the rafter or lookout locations. If necessary, finish the cut with a wood chisel.

2 Remove the damaged soffit section, using a flat pry bar if necessary. Cut nailing strips and attach them to the rafters or rafter lookouts at the edges of the opening (step 2, next page).

3 Measure the opening, and cut a soffit patch to fit from material similar to the original soffit. Allow ⅛" on all sides for expansion gaps. Make cutouts for existing soffit vents, or for new soffit vents (page 54).

4 Install the soffit patch by driving 1¼" galvanized deck screws into the nailing strips or rafter lookouts. NOTE: If you do not plan to paint the entire soffit, you may find it easier to prime and paint the patch before installing.

5 Reattach the soffit molding, using 4d galvanized casing nails.

6 Fill nail holes, screw holes, and gaps with siliconized acrylic caulk. Smooth out the caulk so it is even with the surface. Prime and paint to match. Install vent covers if needed.

How to Repair Tongue-and-groove Soffits

1 Remove the soffit molding. Locate the closest rafter lookout on each side of the damaged area. Drill an entry hole for a jig saw, then cut out the damaged section, cutting as close as possible to the lookout. Pry the damaged section loose. NOTE: To remove width-run tongue-and-groove soffits (inset), cut across the ends of boards near the fascia.

2 Cut a nailing strip from 2 × 2 stock, and fasten it to the rafter lookout at each end of the opening, using 2½" galvanized deck screws.

3 Cut patch boards to fit, using similar tongue-and-groove stock. Fasten all but the final board by driving 8d galvanized casing nails through pilot holes in the tongues of the boards, and into the nailing strips. Set the nail heads so the next patch board will fit cleanly over the tongue of the first board.

Top lip removed

4 Trim the top lip from grooved edge of the final board in the installation sequence. Position the board in the opening. Face-nail ring-shank siding nails through the last patch board and into the nailing strips. Prime and paint to match. Attach soffit vents covers, if needed.

Rehanging sagging gutters is a common gutter repair. Before rehanging, snap a chalk line that follows the original slope (usually about ¼" per 10 ft. toward the downspouts). To rehang gutters, remove the hangers in and near the sag, and lift the gutter until it is flush with the chalk line. Reattach the hangers (replace them if they are in bad condition), shifting their location slightly so you do not use the original holes. If the hangers are more than 24" apart, or there is no hanger within 12" of a seam, add hangers.

Repairing Gutters

Gutters channel water away from your home. Clogged, sagging, or leaky gutters can cause extensive damage to your siding, foundation, or landscaping. They can also result in water buildup in your basement.

Evaluate the type and extent of gutter damage to select the appropriate repair method. Often, small leaks and minor damage can be repaired with easy-to-use gutter repair products (next page). Moderate damage to metal gutters can be patched with flashing (pages 48 to 49). TIP: Prevent corrosion by patching with the same type of metal (usually aluminum or galvanized steel) from which the gutters are made.

If the damaged area is more than 2 ft. in length, replace the entire section of gutter with new material (page 49). To locate a section of gutter for making repairs, trace the profile of your existing gutters and take it with you to the building center. Also measure the gutter at the widest point—if your gutters are more than 15 years old, they likely are a little larger than gutters made today. Check salvage yards, or have a new section custom-bent by a metal fabricator.

If your gutters are beyond repair, remove and replace them. Snap-together vinyl gutters (pages 50 to 51) are popular with today's homeowners.

If your house has wood gutters, patch small holes or rot with epoxy wood filler (pages 14 to 15). If damage is more serious, contact a professional carpenter.

Everything You Need:

Tools: utility knife, stiff-bristled or wire brush, abrasive pads, aviator snips, screwdriver, pry bar, hammer, portable drill, hacksaw, caulk gun.

Materials: gutter caulk, gutter patching kit, roof cement, flashing material, gutter fasteners.

Gutter Accessories

Install gutter guards to prevent buildup of debris in the gutters. Buy guards that match the size and style of your gutters. Common mesh gutter guards (above) usually require mesh supports. **Downspout strainers** at the outlets prevent debris from collecting in downspouts, where clogs are hard to remove.

Install a swing-up elbow at the end of each drain pipe, allowing the outlet pipe to be lifted out of the way when you are working near the foundation of the house. Add a **splash block** to prevent erosion and help direct runoff away from your house.

Tips for Using Gutter Repair Products

Use gutter caulk to fill small holes and seal minor leaks. Usually made with a butyl-rubber base, gutter caulk flexes without losing its seal. It is also resistant to the elements.

Use gutter patching kits for temporary repairs to gutters with minor damage. Read the manufacturer's recommendations and directions before purchasing and using repair products. For long-term repairs, see pages 48 to 49.

How to Patch Metal Gutters

1 Clean the area around the damage with a wire brush. Scrub with an abrasive pad to loosen residue, then clean the area with water.

2 Apply a ⅛"-thick layer of roof cement evenly over the damage, and spread it a few inches beyond the damaged area on all sides.

3 Cut and bend a patch from flashing made from the same material as the gutters. Bed the patch in the roof cement, and feather the cement so it will not cause significant damming.

How to Repair Leaky Joints

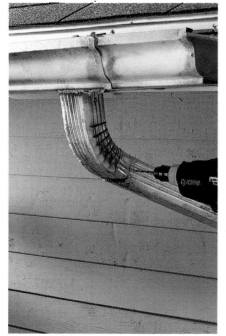

1 Drill out rivets or remove metal screws that secure the joint. Disassemble the damaged joint. With downspouts, you may need to disassemble the entire downspout to get the bad joint apart.

2 Scrub both parts of the joint, using a stiff-bristled brush (for vinyl gutters) or a wire brush (for metal gutters). Clean the damaged area with water.

3 When dry, apply caulk to the joining parts, then reassemble the joint. Reinforce with new fasteners, adding new hangers if the originals need replacing.

How to Replace a Section of Metal Gutter

Protective spacer

1 Remove gutter hangers in or near the damaged area. TIP: Insert wood spacers in the gutter, near each hanger, before putting pressure on the gutter. This helps protect gutters from damage.

2 Slip spacers between the gutter and fascia, near each end of the damaged area, so you do not damage the roof when cutting the gutter. Cut out the damaged area with a hacksaw.

3 Cut a gutter patch from material similar in type, size, and profile to the original gutter. The patch should be at least 4" longer than the damaged section.

4 With a wire brush, clean the cut ends of the old gutter. Caulk the ends, then center the gutter patch over the damage and press into caulk.

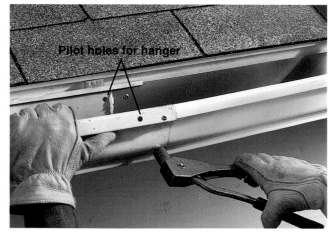

Pilot holes for hanger

5 Secure the gutter patch with pop rivets or sheet metal screws. Use at least three or four fasteners at each joint. On the inside surfaces of the gutter, caulk over the heads of the fasteners.

6 Install the gutter hangers, using new hangers if necessary (do not use old holes). Prime and paint the patch to match.

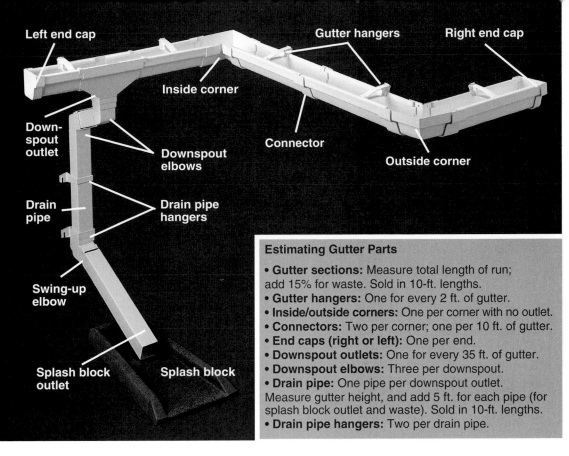

Left end cap

Gutter hangers

Right end cap

Inside corner

Down-spout outlet

Downspout elbows

Connector

Outside corner

Drain pipe

Drain pipe hangers

Swing-up elbow

Splash block outlet

Splash block

Vinyl snap-together gutter systems are becoming increasingly popular. Easy to install and relatively inexpensive, they will not rot or deteriorate. The slip joints allow for expansion and contraction. Before you purchase and install new gutters, make a cost estimate. Do not base the estimate solely on the advertised prices of gutter and drain pipe sections, which make up only a fraction of the final cost of the system.

Estimating Gutter Parts

- **Gutter sections:** Measure total length of run; add 15% for waste. Sold in 10-ft. lengths.
- **Gutter hangers:** One for every 2 ft. of gutter.
- **Inside/outside corners:** One per corner with no outlet.
- **Connectors:** Two per corner; one per 10 ft. of gutter.
- **End caps (right or left):** One per end.
- **Downspout outlets:** One for every 35 ft. of gutter.
- **Downspout elbows:** Three per downspout.
- **Drain pipe:** One pipe per downspout outlet. Measure gutter height, and add 5 ft. for each pipe (for splash block outlet and waste). Sold in 10-ft. lengths.
- **Drain pipe hangers:** Two per drain pipe.

Installing a Vinyl Snap-together Gutter System

Installing a new gutter system is a manageable task for most homeowners. Snap-together gutter systems are designed for ease of installation, requiring no fasteners other than the screws used to attach the gutter hangers to the fascia.

Draw a detailed plan before purchasing and installing new gutters. See the chart above for tips on planning and estimating. If you have never installed gutters before, you may find it

helpful to test-fit all the pieces on the ground, following your plan, before you begin the actual installation.

Everything You Need:

Tools: chalk line, tape measure, drill, hacksaw.

Materials: 1¼" deck screws, gutters and drain pipes, connectors, and fittings (see above).

How to Install Vinyl Snap-together Gutters

Slope= ¼" per 10 ft.

Fascia

1 Mark a point at the high end of each gutter run, 1" down from the top of the fascia. Snap chalk lines that slope ¼" per 10 ft. toward downspout outlets. For runs longer than 35 ft., mark a slope from a high point in the center toward downspouts at each end.

2 Install downspout outlets near the ends of gutter runs (at least one outlet for every 35 ft. of run). The tops of the outlets should be flush with the slope line, and they should align with end caps on the corners of your house, where drain pipes will be attached.

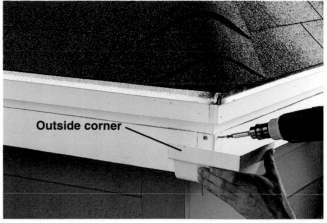

3 Attach hangers or support clips for hangers (some models) for a complete run, following the manufacturer's directions. Attach to fascia at 24" intervals, using 1¼" deck screws. Follow the slope line.

4 Attach outside and inside corners at corner locations that do not have downspout outlets or end caps. Follow the slope line.

5 Cut gutter sections to fit between outlets and corners, using a hacksaw. Attach end cap, and connect gutter section to outlet. Cut gutter sections to fit between outlets, allowing for expansion gaps. Test-fit.

6 On the ground, join the gutter sections together using connectors. Attach gutter hangers to the gutters (for models with support clips mounted on fascia). Hang the gutters, connecting to the outlets.

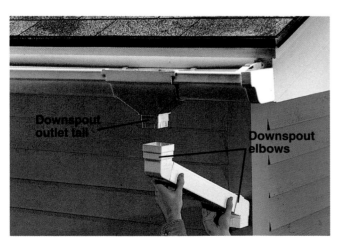

7 Cut a section of drain pipe to fit between two downspout elbows—one elbow should fit over the tail of the downspout outlet, the other fits against the wall. Assemble the parts, slip the top elbow onto the outlet, and secure the other with a drain pipe hanger.

8 Cut a piece of drain pipe to fit between the elbow at the top of the wall (step 7) and the end of the drain pipe run (at least 12" above the ground). Attach an elbow to the end of the pipe, and secure to the wall with a drain-pipe hanger. Add accessories (page 47).

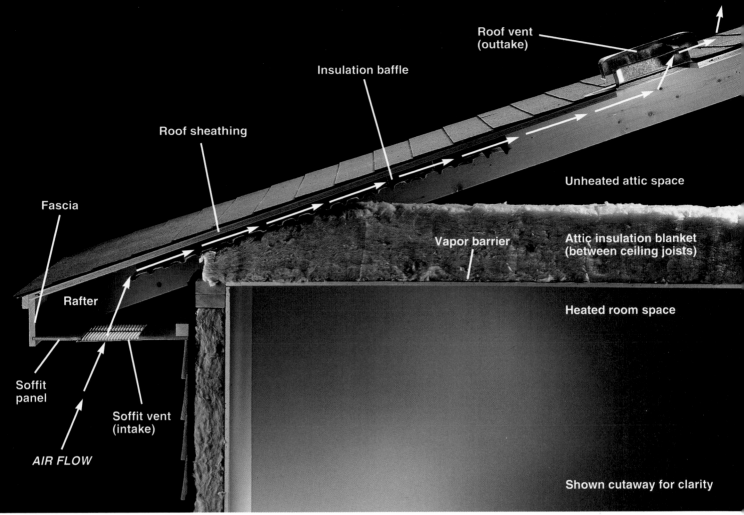

Roof vent
(outtake)

Insulation baffle

Roof sheathing

Unheated attic space

Fascia

Vapor barrier

Attic insulation blanket
(between ceiling joists)

Rafter

Heated room space

Soffit
panel

Soffit vent
(intake)

AIR FLOW

Shown cutaway for clarity

Sufficient air flow prevents heat build-up in your attic, and helps protect your roof from damage caused by condensation or ice. A typical ventilation system has vents in the soffits to admit fresh air, which flows upward beneath the roof sheathing and exits through roof vents.

Installing Soffit & Roof Vents

An effective ventilation system equalizes temperatures on both sides of the roof, which helps keep your house cooler in the summer and prevents ice dams at the roof eaves in cold climates.

The best strategy for increasing roof ventilation is to add more of the existing types of vents. If you are reroofing, however, consider replacing all your roof vents with a continuous ridge vent (next page). You can increase outtake ventilation by replacing a standard roof vent with an electric turbine vent, but an easier solution is simply to add another standard roof vent.

Everything You Need:

Tools: hammer, caulk gun, drill, jig saw, tape measure, pry bar, pencil, utility knife.
Materials: roofing nails, roof cement, stainless steel screws, soffit vent covers, roof vents.

Determining Ventilation Requirements

Measure attic floor space to determine how much ventilation you need. You should have one square foot each of intake and outtake vents for every 150 square feet of unheated attic floor space.

Common Intake Ventilation Types

Soffit vents can be added to increase air flow into attics on houses with a closed soffit system. Make sure there is an unobstructed air passage from the soffit area to the roof before you install new soffit vents (page 54).

Continuous soffit vents provide even air flow into attics. They are usually installed during new construction, but they can be added as retrofits to unvented soffit panels.

Common Outtake Ventilation Types

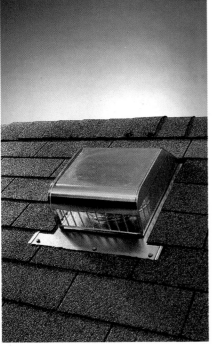

Roof vents can be added near the ridge line when you need to increase outtake ventilation. Fixed roof vents are easy to install (page 55) and have no mechanical parts that can break down.

Gable and dormer vents generally are installed instead of soffit vents—especially on houses with open eaves. Covers come in a variety of styles and colors to match siding.

Continuous ridge vents create an even outtake air flow because they span the entire ridge. Barely noticeable from the ground, ridge vents are usually installed during roof construction, but can be added during a reroofing project.

How to Install a Soffit Vent

1 Examine the eave area from inside your attic to make sure there is nothing obstructing air flow from the soffits. If insulation is blocking the air passage, install insulation baffles (page 76).

2 Draw a cutout for the soffit vent cover on the soffit panel. Center the vents between the fascia and the side of the house. The cover outline should be ¼" smaller on all sides than the soffit vent cover.

3 Drill a starter hole, then cut the vent openings with a jig saw.

4 Caulk the flanges of the vent cover with siliconized acrylic caulk. Screw the vent cover to the soffit.
TIP: For visual effect, install all of the new vent covers with the louvers pointing in the same direction.

How to Install a Roof Vent

1 Mark the location for the roof vent by driving a nail through the roof sheathing. The nail should be centered between rafters, and between 16" and 24" from the ridge pole.

2 Locate the marker nail, and center the vent cover over the nail. Outline the base flange of the vent cover on the shingles, then remove shingles in an area 2" inside the outline. Mark the roof-vent hole using the marker nail as a centerpoint. Cut the hole with a reciprocating saw or jig saw.

3 Apply roof cement to the underside of the base flange. Set the vent cover in position, slipping the base flange under the shingles, centered over the vent-hole cutout.

4 Secure the roof vent to the sheathing with rubber gasket nails on all sides of the flange. Tack down any loose shingles. Do not nail through the base flange when attaching shingles.

Repairing Siding & Trim

The materials we use to cover the outside of our home have changed dramatically in recent years. But even with the advances, one fact has not changed: all types of siding and trim need some maintenance or repair from time to time.

Traditional wood lap siding can be repaired quite easily if, like most homeowners, you have some experience repairing wood. Epoxy-based wood fillers and long-lasting caulk products make the task easy. And replacing missing or damaged wood shakes is one of the simplest exterior home repairs.

Repairing masonry siding, like brick veneer and stucco, no longer requires a skilled mason. It can be repaired with a few easy-to-apply products (pages 118 to 119).

But perhaps the most significant change in siding maintenance and repair has come with "low-maintenance" or "no-maintenance" manufactured siding products. Once viewed as gimmicks sold door-to-door, aluminum, vinyl, and steel siding products have become commonplace in the past few decades. When they first hit the market, repair of these products was the exclusive terrain of licensed contractors, but now most building centers carry a range of replacement parts and repair products. As a result, simple repairs can be done by do-it-yourselfers.

However, there are still some repairs you should think twice about attempting. If the damage to your siding (whatever its type) is so extensive that it appears to require full replacement, you should consider hiring a contractor. Few home improvement projects are more time-consuming than applying new siding—especially if you are installing products that you have never worked with before. There is a lot of competition among siding contractors, and you can usually come up with a range of bids. But do not look only at the cost—whenever hiring a contractor, check references and licenses, and get estimates in writing.

This section shows:

Siding damage, like the water damage caused by the leaky hose bib shown above, often requires replacement of the affected siding pieces. Identify and eliminate the cause of the damage before you replace or repair siding and trim (pages 8 and 99).

Evaluating Siding & Trim

The first step in inspecting and evaluating siding and trim is to identify with certainty the material types (photos, below). Once you have determined the material, take a closer look for any potential problems (photos, right). If your siding is under warranty, read the warranty document closely before attempting any repairs. Making repairs yourself could invalidate the product warranty.

CAUTION: many homes built in the 1940s and 1950s were covered with milled asbestos shingles. Asbestos shingles have the same general appearance as fiberglass, usually with a rough, heavily ridged surface. Because asbestos is classified as a hazardous material, its handling and disposal are regulated. Contact your local waste management department before handling asbestos shingles.

Common Siding Types

Wood lap siding is usually made of cedar, pine, or hardwood particle board. Beveled boards are the most common. Wood lap is very easy to repair (pages 62 to 64).

Vinyl siding is virtually maintenance-free. Minor repairs can be made with caulk or patches (pages 66 to 67). Contact a siding contractor before making major repairs.

Metal siding: Minor patching and caulking can take care of many common problems affecting metal siding (pages 66 to 67). Contact a contractor for major repairs.

Shakes & shingles: Shakes (shown) and shingles usually are cut from cedar or pine. Basic repairs are easy on wood shakes and shingles (pages 64).

Brick: Small problems in brick veneer can be repaired with quick-fix concrete repair products (pages 118 to 119). For major repairs, contact an expert.

Stucco: Minor repairs, like filling thin cracks or small holes, can be made with concrete or stucco repair products (page 65). For wide cracks and major damage, call an expert.

Common Siding Problems

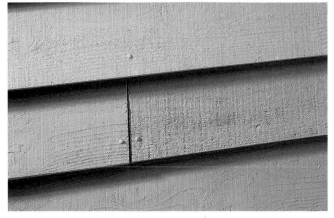

Separated joints can occur in any type of lap siding, but are most common in wood lap. Gaps between ⅛" and ¼" thick can be filled with caulk. Gaps ⅜" or wider could mean that your house has a serious moisture or shifting problem: consult a professional inspector.

Buckling occurs most frequently in manufactured siding, when expansion gaps are too small at the points where the siding fits into trim and channels. If possible, move the channel slightly. If not, remove the siding (page 64), trim length slightly, then reinstall.

Minor surface damage to metal siding is best left alone in most cases—unless damage has penetrated the surface (page 61). With metal products, cosmetic surface repairs often look worse than the damage.

Missing siding, like the cedar shakes that have been blown from the wall shown above, should be replaced immediately (pages 60 to 67). Check the surrounding siding to make sure it is secure.

Tips for Inspecting Trim

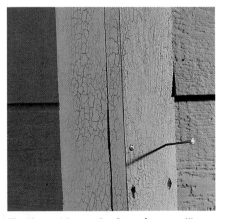

Check window and door trim for rot, especially on horizontal surfaces and at joints. Try to make repairs without removal (pages 68 to 69).

Remove decorative trim, like the gingerbread trim above, if you suspect damage. Inspecting and repairing it is easier in a workshop.

Evaluate broad trim pieces, like the end cap trim shown above, and make repairs using the same techniques used for siding.

Stagger vertical seams to make your siding repairs less visible. Where possible, drive fasteners into framing members. Siding sheathing or underlayment, if present at all, is often made from soft composite boards that do not hold fasteners well.

Repairing Siding

Repairing common types of siding damage is a manageable project for most homeowners. Small to medium-size holes, cracks, and rotted areas can be repaired by filling with repair products or by replacing the damaged sections with matching siding.

As with most exterior repair projects, the primary goal of siding repair is to make sure minor or moderate damage does not turn into major damage. But a well-executed siding repair also will add to the visual appeal of your home, especially if the repair materials are a good blend with the surrounding siding.

If you cannot find new matching siding for patches at building centers, check with salvage yards or siding contractors. When repairing aluminum or vinyl siding, contact the manufacturer or the contractor who installed the siding to help you locate matching materials and parts. If you cannot find an exact match, remove original siding from a less-visible area of your house, like the back of the garage, and use it as the patch. Patch the gap in the less-visible area with the near-match siding.

Tips for Repairing Siding

Create an expansion gap at each seam between wood siding panels or lap siding. Use a nail as a guide to set the width of the gaps (for most siding types, ⅛" is an adequate expansion gap). Fill the gaps with exterior caulk (pages 14 to 15).

Repair small holes with the appropriate filler product. For *wood siding* (top), fill holes with epoxy wood filler. Paint to match. For *metal and vinyl siding* (bottom), use tinted exterior caulk to fill holes. If you cannot find a matching color at a building center, check with the siding manufacturer.

Number the siding pieces as you remove them from your house to simplify reinstallation. You can also use the boards as templates for replacement pieces.

Patch damaged building paper before attaching new siding. When applying a patch, loosen the building paper above the damaged area, and slip the top of the patch underneath. Attach the patch with staples. Use roof cement to patch small holes or tears.

Insert spacers between the siding and sheathing above the work area while you make repairs to lap siding. This creates better access, simplifying the repair process. **CAUTION:** Metal siding will buckle if bent too far.

Repairing Wood Siding

Wood siding is the easiest type to repair. Fixing cracks, replacing damaged sections, and filling holes requires only basic carpentry tools and inexpensive materials. Only use wood and wood repair products that are suitable for exterior use.

Everything You Need:

Tools: hammer, chisel, trowel, screwdrivers, hacksaw, circular saw, keyhole saw, pry bar, nail set, electronic stud finder, paint brush.

Materials: epoxy wood filler, epoxy glue, nails and deck screws, siliconized acrylic caulk, plastic roof cement, building paper, lumber crayon, sheathing, wood preservative, primer, paint or stain.

Repair cracks and splits in wood siding with epoxy wood glue. Apply the glue to both sides of the crack, then press the board back together. For best results, position a board under the bottom edge of the damaged board and press it upward to create even pressure until the glue sets (if working near the ground, wedge a 2 × 4 under the board). After the glue sets, drive galvanized deck screws on each side of the crack to reinforce the repair. Clean off excess glue, and touch up the repair with paint.

How to Replace a Section of Wood Lap Siding

1 Using an electronic stud finder, locate and mark framing members around the repair area. Mark cutout lines over the centers of framing members on each side of the repair area. Stagger the lines so vertical joints do not align (page 60, top photo).

2 Insert spacers beneath the board above the repair area. Make entry cuts at the tops of the cutting lines with a keyhole saw, then saw through the boards with the saw in an upright position. Remove the boards. Pry out any nails, or cut off the heads with a hacksaw blade.

TIP: Trace cutouts for any fixtures, wall openings, or other obstructions using the old siding board as a template. Also mark the end lines if the template board is still intact (make sure there will be a ⅛"-wide expansion gap at each end). Make the cutouts with a jig saw or coping saw, then cut to length.

3 Measure and cut all replacement siding boards to fit, leaving an expansion gap of ⅛" at each end. Apply wood preservative/sealer or primer to the ends and back sides of the boards before installation.

4 Nail the new boards in place with ring-shank siding nails, starting with the lowest board. Drive nails into framing members using the original nailing pattern (normally at 12" intervals through the bottom of the exposed board and the top of the board below).

5 Fill expansion joints with caulk (use paintable caulk for painted wood, and tinted caulk for stained wood), then prime and paint or stain the replacement siding boards to match the surrounding boards.

How to Replace Wood Shakes & Shingles

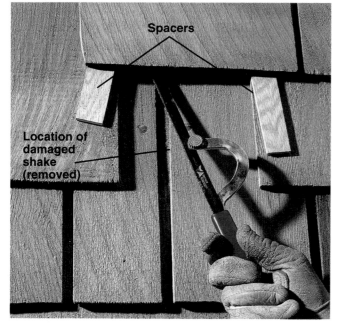

1 Split damaged shakes or shingles with a hammer and chisel, and remove. Insert wood spacers under the shakes or shingles above the repair area, then slip a hacksaw blade under the top board to cut off any nail heads remaining from the old shake or shingle.

2 Cut replacement shakes or shingles to fit, leaving a ⅛" to ¼"-wide expansion gap at each side. Coat all sides and edges with wood preservative. Slip the patch pieces under the siding above the repair area (start on lower courses if patching a large area). Attach with ring-shank siding nails, driven near the top of the exposed area on the patch. Cover nail heads with caulk, wiping off any excess. Remove spacers.

How to Replace Siding Panels

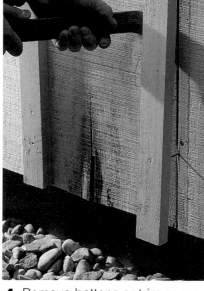

1 Remove battens or trim securing the damaged panels. Pry out the entire damaged panel. Inspect the building paper under the panels, and patch as needed.

2 Cut replacement panels from matching material, allowing a ⅛"-wide expansion gap at side seams. Prime or seal the edges and back side of the replacement boards before installing.

3 Nail the new boards in place with ring-shank siding nails. Caulk all seams and expansion joints, then replace battens and other trim. Prime and paint or stain to match.

Repairing Stucco

Stucco is a very long-lasting siding product. But, over time, it will crumble and crack. Making permanent repairs to extensively damaged stucco walls is a job for a professional, but most homeowners can make smaller repairs with simple repair products.

Use premixed stucco repair compound for patching small holes or crumbled areas in stucco walls. Use concrete or stucco repair caulk for filling small cracks. For other masonry repair products, see pages 118 to 119.

Everything You Need:

Tools: wire brush, putty knife, whisk broom.

Materials: concrete caulk, stucco repair compound.

Fill thin cracks with concrete caulk. Overfill the crack with caulk, and feather until it is flush with the stucco. Allow the caulk to set, then paint to match. Concrete caulk stays semiflexible, preventing further cracking.

How to Patch Stucco Walls

1 Clean out loose material from the repair area with a wire brush. Remove rust from any exposed metal lath, and treat the lath with metal primer.

2 Trowel premixed stucco repair compound into the repair area with a putty knife or pointed trowel, overfilling slightly (read manufacturer's directions—drying times and application techniques vary).

3 Smooth out the repair with a putty knife or trowel, feathering it even with the surrounding surface. Use a whisk broom to create a matching texture on the stucco patch. Touch up with masonry paint to blend in the repair.

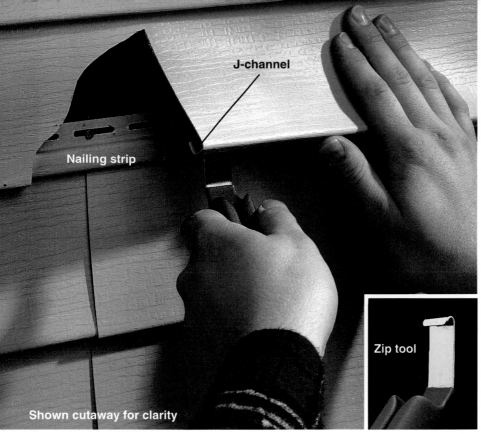

J-channel

Nailing strip

Zip tool

Shown cutaway for clarity

Repairing Vinyl & Metal Siding

Vinyl and metal siding are popular with homeowners because they are inexpensive and can last for decades. However, the materials are susceptible to dents, holes, and fading. Minor repairs can be done by do-it-yourselfers. For major work, and to help find replacement parts, contact the contractor that installed your siding, or the siding manufacturer.

Everything You Need:

Tools: hammer, tape measure, drill, aviator snips, utility knife, caulk gun, zip tool, pry bar, straightedge.

Materials: nails; caulk; roof cement or exterior panel adhesive; end caps, trim, and siding panels as needed.

Vinyl and metal siding pieces have a locking J-channel that fits over the bottom of the nailing strip on the piece below. Use a zip tool (inset) to separate siding panels. Insert the zip tool at the overlapping seam nearest the repair area. Slide the zip tool over the J-channel, pulling outward slightly, to unlock the joint from the siding below.

How to Patch Vinyl Siding

Nailing strip trimmed off at overlap

Replacement piece

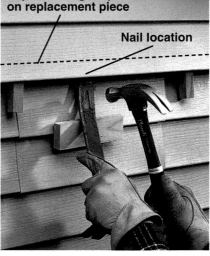

Top of nailing strip on replacement piece

Nail location

1 Unlock interlocking joints with the siding above the repair area, using a zip tool (photo above). Start unlocking at the seam nearest the damaged area. Install spacers below the piece above, then pry out fasteners in the top piece of damaged siding, using a flat pry bar.

2 Cut out the damaged area, using a straightedge and utility knife; then cut a replacement piece 4" longer than the open area, from similar siding material. Before installing, trim off 2" of the nailing strip from each end of the replacement piece in the overlap area. Slide the piece into position.

3 Attach the replacement siding. Because the nailing strip is difficult to reach with a hammer, press ring-shank siding nails in the slots of the nailing strip, then position the end of a flat pry bar over each nail head. Drive nails by rapping on the neck of the pry bar with a hammer. Slip the J-channel over the nailing strip (photo, top left).

How to Patch Metal Siding

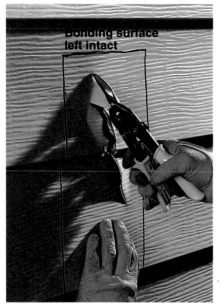

1 Cut out the damaged area with aviator snips and a hacksaw blade. Leave some exposed surface area at the top of the uppermost piece you remove to serve as a bonding surface for the top siding patch.

2 Cut a patch or patches 4" wider than the repair area, using matching material. Cut off the nailing strip from the top of the top patch piece. Make sure all edges are smooth, deburring with metal sandpaper if necessary.

3 Nail lower patches in place by driving ring-shank siding nails through the nailing strips, starting with the lowest piece. To install the top piece, apply roof cement to the back, and press the patch in place, slipping the J-shaped locking channel over the nailing strip below. Caulk the seams.

How to Replace Aluminum End Caps

1 Remove the damaged end cap. If end caps cannot be removed easily, pry the bottom loose, then cut along the top with a hacksaw.

2 Attach replacement end caps, starting at the bottom. Drive ring-shank siding nails through the nailing tabs, and into framing members.

3 Trim the nailing tabs off the top replacement cap, then apply roof cement to the back. Snap the cap over the J-shaped locking channels of the siding courses. Press the top cap securely in place.

Repair delicate or ornamental trim molding in your workshop. You will get better results more easily than if you try repairing it while it is still attached. Leave decorative trim in place if you must remove siding to gain access to it.

Repairing Trim

Some exterior trim serves as decoration, like gingerbread and ornate cornice moldings. Other trim, like brick molding and end caps, works with siding to seal your house from the elements. Damaged brick molding and corner boards should be patched with stock material similar to the original. If you cannot find matching replacement parts for decorative trim, check salvage shops or contact a custom millworker.

Everything You Need:

Tools: hammer, chisel, circular saw, nail set, putty knife, utility knife, paint brush, flat pry bar.

Materials: epoxy wood filler, epoxy glue, caulk, nails and screws, sandpaper, paint, building paper, drip edge.

Tips for Repairing & Replacing Trim

Reattach loose trim with new ring-shank siding nails driven near old nail locations. Fill old nail holes with paintable caulk, and touch up caulk and new nail heads with paint to match the surrounding surface.

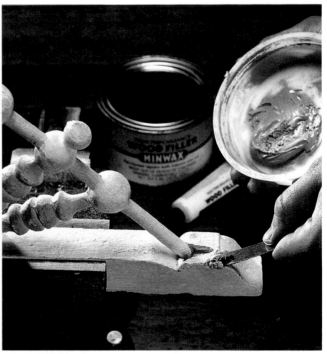

Repair decorative trim molding with epoxy glue or wood filler (page 14). For major repairs, make your own replacement parts, or take the trim to a custom millwork shop.

How to Replace Brick Molding

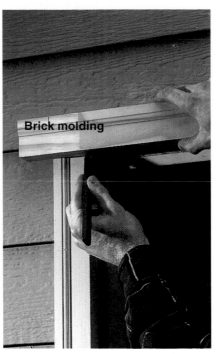

1 Pry off old brick molding around windows and doors using a flat pry bar. Remove any old drip edge. Inspect and repair the building paper (page 61). NOTE: Drip edge that fits above doors and windows is a different product from roof-style drip edge (page 23).

2 Hold a replacement piece of brick molding, slightly longer than the original piece, across the opening. Mark cutting lines to fit the opening. Cut the replacement brick molding at the cutting lines, matching any miter cuts.

3 Cut a 3"-wide piece of flashing to fit between the jambs, then bend it in half lengthwise to form the new drip edge (preformed drip edge is available). Slip it between the siding and the building paper, above the door or window. Do not nail the drip edge in place.

4 Test-fit the replacement piece of brick molding, then apply exterior-grade panel adhesive to the back side. Follow the manufacturer's directions for allowing the adhesive to set.

5 Nail the brick molding to the door header with 10d galvanized casing nails. Lock-nail the miter joints, and set all nail heads. Seal joints, and cover nail holes with caulk. Prime and paint when the caulk dries.

Insulating & Weatherizing

Whether you live in a warm or cold climate, adequately weatherizing and insulating your house has many benefits. It saves money—even in homes with average insulation, heating and cooling costs account for over half of the total energy bill. And because most insulating and weatherstripping products are relatively inexpensive, an investment in them can be recovered through energy savings in a short amount of time.

Also, by reducing energy use, you help reduce pollution and slow the depletion of irreplaceable natural resources. In an average home in a cold climate, it is estimated, reducing energy usage by only 15% can save the equivalent of 500 pounds of coal each year.

And finally, a tightly sealed, well-insulated house not only saves money and resources, it eliminates drafts and cold spots, creating a more comfortable home for your family to enjoy.

This section shows:

- Detecting Energy Loss (pages 72 to 73)
- Insulating & Weatherizing Products (pages 74 to 75)
- Improving Insulation (pages 76 to 79)
- Weatherizing Your House (pages 80 to 87)
- Maintaining Storm Doors & Windows (pages 88 to 94)
- Replacing Storm Windows (page 95)

Obtain an infrared photograph of your house to help identify heat loss. The owner of the house to the right was experiencing high heating bills, and contacted his local public utility company. He was referred to an infrared inspection service, which took the infrared photograph shown above. The photo clearly showed high heat loss (seen as red and yellow in the photo) around his entry door and second-floor window. With this information, he was able to make efficient weatherstripping improvements that paid off quickly.

Detecting Energy Loss

Some signs that your home is not energy efficient are very obvious: for example, general draftiness; windows that are constantly frosted; a roof that loses its snow cover well before other roofs in the neighborhood; and high heating bills. Other signs are trickier to detect; for example, inadequate wall insulation; warm air loss around chimneys; and heat transfer through glass. The tips on these pages will help you detect and solve energy loss problems.

Some energy-loss problems can be expensive and time-consuming to correct: for example, removing interior wall surfaces to improve wall insulation. Check with a contractor, and compare potential savings to the project cost before you undertake any large projects, like adding insulation to finished walls.

Measure insulation between joists in unheated attics to see if amounts meet recommended standards (page 76). Multiply the number of inches of loose insulation by 3.7 to find the total current R-value. For fiberglass insulation, multiply by 3.1 per inch. If the total amounts are substandard, add enough insulation to meet the recommendation (pages 77 to 79).

Tests for Detecting Energy Loss

Measure the temperature in different parts of a room. Differences of more than one or two degrees indicate that the room is poorly sealed. Update weatherstripping around doors and windows (pages 82 to 87).

Check for drafts around windows and doors by holding a tissue next to gaps at the door or window on a windy day. Fluttering indicates weatherstripping is inadequate, and it should be replaced or upgraded (pages 82 to 87). Also look for light coming from the outside around door and window jambs.

Conduct an energy audit with the assistance of your local public utility company. Most power companies will provide an energy audit kit, or conduct the audit for you (sometimes free of charge). Some audits include the use of a blower door (above), which measures air flow and detects leakage.

Tips for Identifying Energy Loss

Frost buildup on windows is a sign of poor weather-stripping and an inadequate storm window. If a tight seal is not made, cold air surrounds the window, causing moisture in the warm inside air to condense on the surface of the cold glass. As moisture builds up, it turns to frost or even ice. Upgrade weatherstripping and add a layer of plastic sheeting on the interior or exterior side of the window (page 74).

Condensation or frost between windows indicates that moisture is building up in the space between the window and the storm window. Fix the problem by updating interior weatherstripping to keep warm, moist air inside (pages 82 to 84). Also check the storm window to make sure there is an outlet for moisture. If not, drill one or two small holes in the lower rail of the storm window so moisture can escape (page 84).

Inspect weatherstripping and insulation. Look for signs of deterioration: crumbling foam or rubber; hardening of flexible products, like felt or foam rubber; or damaged metal stripping. Replace the products as needed. Most weatherstripping products will last only a few years.

Monitor energy usage and costs and compare them year-to-year, taking into account any changes in the rate structures or general weather conditions. Significant increases may indicate that weatherstripping or insulation needs replacement or improvement. Make further evaluations to determine where energy loss is occurring—like having an infrared photo taken of your home (page 71).

Insulating & Weatherizing Products

(A) A vapor barrier prevents condensation from occurring around insulation. Use 6-mil poly as a vapor barrier for rigid insulation boards or unfaced fiberglass insulation (page 76).

(B) Faced fiberglass insulation has an attached vapor barrier. More expensive than unfaced insulation, it is especially useful in areas, like crawl spaces, where the vapor barrier must be on the opposite side from which the insulation is installed.

(C) An attic blanket is a common type of unfaced fiberglass insulation. Unfaced insulation is less costly than faced insulation and, when used with a solid poly vapor barrier, it provides better protection from mois-

ture. Sold in rolls and flat batts sized to fit standard stud cavities.

(D) Rigid insulation boards are attached directly to basement walls, usually with panel adhesive. Urethane foam insulation (shown) is sturdy and a good insulator. Inexpensive open-cell foam boards can be used, but they are harder to work with. Rigid boards are sold in thicknesses ranging from ½" to 2".

(E) Baffles are attached to the rafters at the sill plate in your attic. Usually made of plastic or polystyrene, they ensure that attic insulation does not obstruct the air flow across the underside of the roof.

(F) A door sweep attaches to the inside of the door bottom to seal out drafts. Felt (shown) and bristle sweeps work well with uneven floors or low thresholds. Vinyl and rubber versions are also sold.

(G) A threshold insert seals the gap between the door and the threshold. Usually made from vinyl or rubber, most can be replaced easily. **A door bottom** fits around the bottom of the door. Most have a sweep on the interior side and a drip edge on the exterior to direct water away from the threshold.

(H) Metal v-channel forms a seal between sliding window sash (shown), in sash channels, or between doors and jambs. Metal v-channel is similar to tension stripping (page 86).

(I) A garage-door sweep creates a continuous barrier between the garage door and the garage floor.

(J) Tubular gasket flexes to cover gaps between moving parts, like window sash. It also can be used on door and window stops because it is compressible.

(K) Switch and receptacle sealers fit behind cover plates on exterior walls to block drafts in these heat-loss areas.

(L) Self-adhesive foam strips are attached to sash and window or door frames where contact occurs with windows and doors.

(M) Reinforced felt strips have a metal spine to add rigidity for high-impact areas, like door stops.

(N) Plastic sheeting adds an extra storm window layer. Interior and exterior types are sold. Interior (shown) can be made wrinkle-free by warming with a hair dryer.

(O) Peelable caulk is applied in gaps around windows and doors, on the interior side. It can be peeled off easily at the end of the heating season.

(P) Caulk can be applied on interior or exterior surfaces to fill narrow gaps. See pages 14 to 15.

(Q) Caulking backer rope fills large voids and gaps that are difficult to caulk. It can be used alone to fill wider gaps.

(R) Sprayable foam is sprayed into hard-to-reach areas, like siding cutouts and baseboard gaps. For best control, use foam with a 1:1 expansion rate.

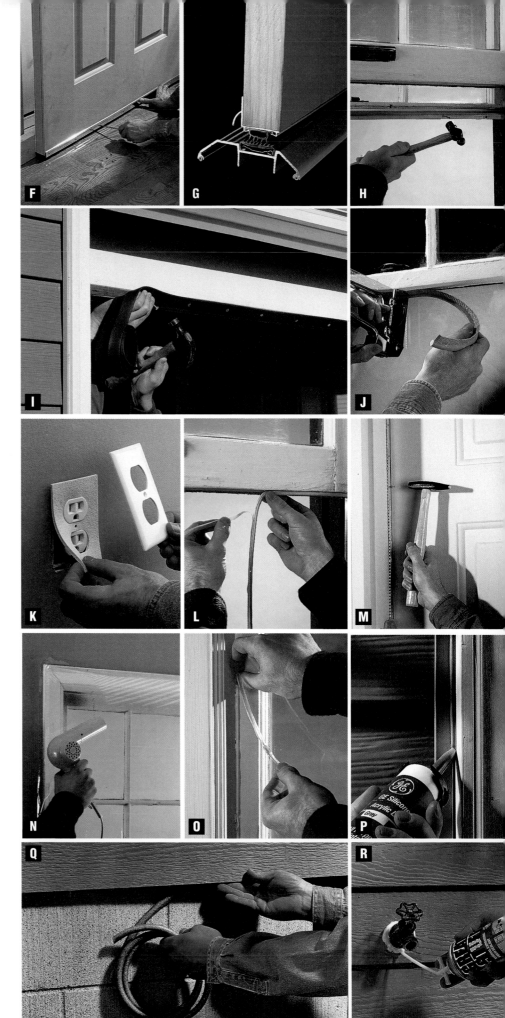

Install baffles to keep new attic insulation from blocking the flow of air through your attic. You can purchase and install ready-made baffles, or make your own from plywood or rigid insulation board. For more information on ventilation, see pages 52 to 55.

Improving Insulation

Adding insulation to attics or basement walls is a quick and easy do-it-yourself project that has an immediate payback in energy savings.

Most local building codes require minimum amounts of insulation for new construction. Check with your building inspector—these minimum requirements make good guidelines for owners of older homes as well. Guidelines for insulation are given in terms of total "R-value," which measures the ability of materials to resist the flow of heat (see chart below).

In this section we show you how to install a fiberglass attic blanket. For most homeowners this is a simpler and cleaner type of attic insulation than loose, blown insulation. Attics with existing insulation should have a vapor barrier in place: use unfaced insulation. Rigid boards are good for basement walls because they pack greater R-value into smaller spaces, and they can be attached directly to walls with panel adhesive.

Everything You Need:

Tools: tape measure, utility knife, straightedge, plumb line, insulation board saw, staple gun.

Materials: 6-mil poly vapor barrier, baffles, insulation, 2 × 2 furring strips, construction adhesive, rigid foam insulation, panel adhesive.

Tips for Planning Your Insulation Project

Recommended insulation amounts		
	Cold climate	**Moderate climate**
Attic:	R38	R26
Wall:	R19	R19
Floor:	R22	R11

Insulation thickness chart:

Fiberglass		Open-cell foam:	
R11 (faced)	3½"	R4	1"
R13 (unfaced)	3½"	R6	1½"
R19 (unfaced)	6"	R8	2"
R21 (high density)	5¼"	**Urethane foam:**	
R25 (unfaced)	8"	R5	1"
R30 (unfaced)	10"	R10	2"

Resistance value (R-value) measures the ability of a material to resist heat flow. The charts above show minimum R-values for different areas (often obtained by combining two layers). Use the lower chart to determine how much insulation you can install in a specific area (never compress insulation).

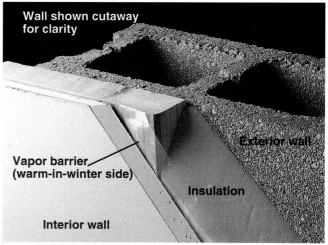

Wall shown cutaway for clarity

Exterior wall

Insulation

Vapor barrier (warm-in-winter side)

Interior wall

Install vapor barriers made of 6-mil (recommended) or 4-mil poly on the warm-in-winter side of insulation. Vapor barriers protect the insulation and the structural members of your house from condensation that can occur when warm, humid air meets cold air. When layering insulation, install one vapor barrier only.

Tips for Insulating Your House

Install fiberglass insulation between floor joists over crawl spaces or unheated basements. Make sure the vapor barrier faces up, and install chicken wire or insulation support rods below to hold the insulation in place.

Insulate the rim joist at the top of your foundation walls by filling it loosely with fiberglass insulation. Pack the insulation just tightly enough that it does not fall out.

Insulate garage walls in attached garages. Use faced fiberglass insulation, with the vapor barrier facing into the garage. Cover with wall covering, like wallboard, especially in areas that are vulnerable to damage.

Tips for Installing Insulation

Insulation Dams

Make insulation dams from rigid boards and install them between ceiling joists to keep attic insulation at least 6" away from recessed lights, vents fans, and other electrical fixtures that generate heat. Check the fixture to see if it is "IC" rated for insulation contact. If it is IC rated, no dams are needed.

Do not compress insulation to fit a spot. Insulation needs air space within the material to be effective in resisting heat transfer. If the insulation you want to install is too thick, trim or tear it to match the depth of the wall, ceiling, or floor cavity.

How to Insulate Your Attic

1 Measure the depth of existing insulation, and calculate how much additional insulation, if any, is required (see page 72 top left, and page 76, chart). TIP: When working over exposed joists, lay a sheet of plywood across the joists to create a stable working surface.

2 Attach baffles to the roof sheathing or rafters to keep new insulation from blocking the air flow along the roof sheathing. Baffles should extend past the bottoms of the ceiling joists.

3 Cut rolls of unfaced fiberglass insulation to length in a well-ventilated work area, using a straightedge and a utility knife. For attics with uneven joist spacing, you will need to trim a few pieces for width as well.

4 Roll out insulation, starting at the farthest point from the attic access. NOTE: Attic blankets may be piled higher than the tops of the joists as long as you do not plan to use your attic for storage.

OPTION: For greater insulation (especially in colder climates), roll out a second attic blanket layer perpendicular to the first layer. Do not use faced insulation or another layer of vapor barrier.

How to Insulate Basement Walls

1 Use a plumb line to mark vertical reference lines for furring strips. Space the furring strips to conform to the width of the rigid insulation boards (do not space them more than 24" apart). Use construction adhesive to attach the furring strips to the foundation walls. OPTION: If you plan to install wallboard over furring strips, attach top and sole plates above and below the furring strips.

2 Cut the rigid panels to fit from floor to ceiling, between furring strips. Use an insulation-board saw. Mark and make cutouts for receptacles, windows, and any other obstructions. For our project, we used 2"-thick urethane foam insulation boards.

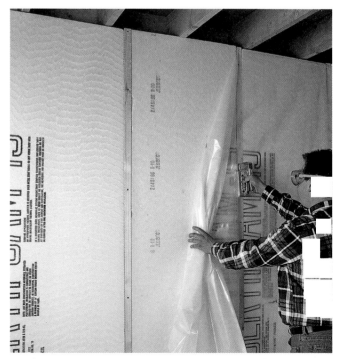

3 Attach the insulation panels to the wall with panel adhesive (check the manufacturer's recommendations to make sure the adhesive is compatible with the type of insulation you purchase).

4 Staple a 6-mil poly vapor barrier to the furring strips. For extra vapor barrier protection, tape over seams and staples with clear plastic tape. Attach wallcovering, if desired.

Cover window wells with preformed window-well covers to minimize heat loss through basement windows (and keep out pests). Most window well covers have an upper flange designed to slip under siding. Fasten them to foundation walls with masonry anchors, and weight down the bottom flange with stones. Caulk around edges for extra protection. Before purchasing window well covers, measure the widest point of your window well, and note whether it is rectangular or semicircular.

Weatherizing Your House

Most weatherizing projects involve windows and doors, because these are the primary heat-loss areas in most homes. Caulk and weatherstripping are the principal tools used to weatherize windows and doors. Storm windows and storm doors also play an important role in weatherizing your home, and similar products, like the plastic window well cover shown above, can make a significant contribution.

Choose weatherstripping materials that meet your specific needs—there are many different types sold, and most are designed for specific applications (page 75). Generally, metal or metal reinforced weatherstripping is more durable than products made from only plastic, rubber, or foam. But even with plastic, rubber, and foam weatherstripping, there is a wide quality range. Neoprene rubber is considered the type of rubber, and should be used whenever it is available.

Weatherizing your house is an ideal project for homeowners because it can be done a little at a time, according to your schedule. The best time to weatherize is in the fall, just before the weather turns too cold to work outdoors.

Tips for Weatherizing Your House

Seal between baseboards and floorboards. Remove the base shoe and spray 1:1-expansion sprayable foam into the gap. While preventing drafts, the foam barrier also stops insects from entering your living areas.

Caulk around dryer vents, exhaust vents from vent fans, and any other fittings mounted to the side of your house.

Insulate around spigots, television cable jacks, telephone lines, and other entry points to your house, using sprayable foam insulation. **CAUTION:** Do not work around or near power service cables.

Seal the sill plate gap between the house sill and the siding by stuffing it with ⅜"-diameter plastic or foam caulking backer rope.

The primary heat loss areas in windows (shown highlighted) should be sealed with the appropriate weatherstripping material. This can increase the energy efficiency of a window by 100% or more.

Weatherizing Windows

The secret to energy-tight windows is blocking air movement, creating a sealed-off dead air space between interior and exterior glass panes.

Modern double and triple-paned windows often contain inert gases between panes to help create dead air spaces. You can create dead air spaces in older windows by using weatherstripping and a good storm window (or plastic window sheeting) to block air movement. Weatherstripping the inside gaps helps keep warm, moist air on the interior side of a window, minimizing condensation and frosting between the window and the storm.

Everything You Need:

Tools: tack hammer, aviator snips, putty knife, hair dryer, staple gun.

Materials: metal v-channel, compressible foam, tubular gasket, reinforced felt, brads, clear silicone caulk, siliconized acrylic caulk, peelable caulk, plastic sheeting (interior and exterior).

How to Weatherstrip Windows

1 Cut metal v-channel to fit in the channels for the sliding sash, extending at least 2" past the closed position for each sash (do not cover sash-closing mechanisms). Attach the v-channel by driving wire brads (usually provided by the manufacturer) with a tack hammer. Drive the fasteners flush with the surface so the sliding sash will not catch on them.

2 Flare out the open ends of the v-channels with a putty knife so the channel is slightly wider than the gap between the sash and the track it fits into. Avoid flaring out too much at one time—it is difficult to press v-channel back together without causing buckling.

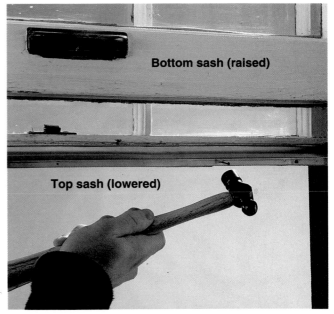

Bottom sash (raised)

Top sash (lowered)

3 Wipe down the underside of the bottom window sash with a damp rag, and let it dry; then, attach self-adhesive compressible foam or rubber to the underside of the sash. Use high-quality hollow neoprene strips, if available. This will create an airtight seal when the window is locked in position.

4 Seal the gap between the top sash and the bottom sash on double-hung windows. Lift the bottom sash and lower the top sash to improve access, and tack metal v-channel to the bottom rail of the top sash using wire brads. TIP: The open end of the "v" should be pointed downward so moisture cannot collect in the channel. Flare out the v-channel with a putty knife to fit the gap between the sash.

Tips for Weatherizing Windows

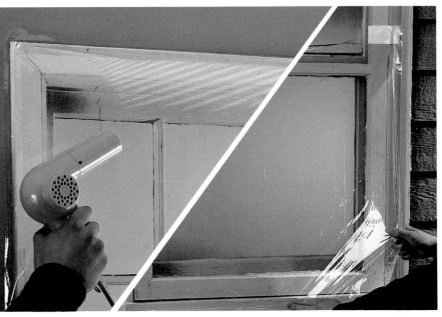

Apply caulk around the interior window casing with clear silicone caulk. For added protection, lock the window in the closed position, and caulk the gaps around the interior edges of the sash with clear, peelable caulk (which can be removed easily when the heating season is over).

Add plastic sheeting or shrink-wrap product to the interior (left photo) to block drafts and keep moisture away from the window surfaces. Follow the manufacturer's installation directions, which often include using a hair dryer to tighten the plastic and remove wrinkles, making it almost invisible. Install exterior plastic sheeting (right photo) on the outside of your window, following the manufacturer's directions (rolls of tacking or stapling strips are often included with the product).

(continued next page)

Tips for Weatherizing Windows (continued)

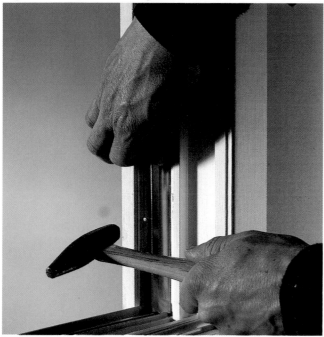

Sliding windows (side by side): Treat side-by-side sliding windows as if they were double-hung windows (pages 82 to 83) turned 90°. For greater durability, substitute metal tension strips for self-adhesive compressible foam in the sash track that fits against the edge of the sash when the window is closed.

Casement windows: Attach self-adhesive foam or rubber compression strips on the outside edges of the window stops.

Tips for Weatherizing Storm Windows

Storm windows: Create a tight seal by attaching foam compression strips to the outside of the storm window stops (left photo). After installing the storm window, fill any gaps between the exterior window trim and the storm window with caulk backer rope. Check the inside surface of the storm window during cold weather for condensation or frost buildup (page 73). If moisture is trapped between the storm window and the permanent window, drill one or two small holes through the bottom rail of the storm window (right photo) to allow moist air to escape. Drill at a slight upward angle.

Weatherizing Doors

Door weatherstripping is prone to failure because it undergoes constant stress. Use metal weatherstripping that is tacked to the surfaces whenever you can—especially around door jambs. It is much more durable than self-adhesive products. If your job calls for flexible weatherstripping, use products made from neoprene rubber, not foam. Replace old door thresholds or threshold inserts as soon as they begin to show wear.

Everything You Need:

Tools: putty knife, tack hammer, screwdriver, backsaw, flat pry bar, chisel and mallet, tape measure, drill.

Materials: metal v-channel or tension strips, reinforced felt strips, door sweep, nails or brads, wood filler, caulk, threshold and insert.

The primary heat loss areas in doors (shown highlighted) are around jambs and at the threshold. Install weatherstripping on jambs, and update the threshold and threshold insert to cut down on drafts.

Tips for Weatherizing Doors

Install a storm door to decrease drafts and energy loss through entry doors. Buy an insulated storm door with a continuous hinge and seamless exterior surface.

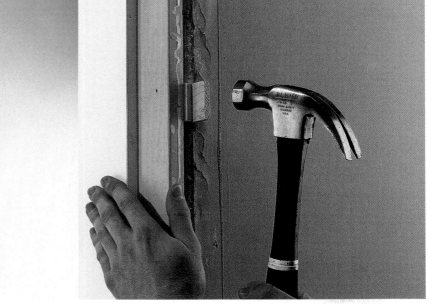

Adjust the door frame to eliminate large gaps between the door and the jamb. Remove the interior case molding and drive new shims between the jamb and the framing member on the hinge side. Close the door to test the fit, and adjust as needed before reattaching case molding. For added home security, install plywood spacers between shims (page 124).

How to Weatherize an Exterior Door

1 Cut two pieces of metal tension strip or v-channel the full height of the door opening, and cut another to full width. Use wire brads to tack the strips to the door jambs and door header, on the interior side of the door stops. TIP: Attach metal weatherstripping from the top down to help prevent buckling. Flare out the tension strips with a putty knife to fill the gaps between the jambs and the door when the door is in closed position (do not pry too far at one time).

2 Add reinforced felt strips to the edge of the door stop, on the exterior side. The felt edge should form a close seal with the door when closed. TIP: Drive fasteners only until they are flush with the surface of the reinforcing spine—overdriving will cause damage and buckling.

3 Attach a new door sweep to the bottom of the door, on the interior side (felt or bristle types are better choices if the floor in your entry area is uneven). Before fastening it permanently, tack the sweep in place and test the door swing to make sure there is enough clearance.

TIP: Fix any cracks in wooden door panels with epoxy wood filler or caulk (page 14) to block air leaks. If the door has a stain finish, use tinted wood putty, filling from the interior side. Sand down and touch up with paint or stain.

How to Replace a Door Threshold

1 Cut the old threshold in two, using a backsaw. Pry out the pieces, and clean the debris from the sill area below the threshold. Note which edge of the threshold is more steeply beveled; the new threshold should be installed in the same way.

2 Measure the opening for the new threshold, and trim it to fit, using the pieces of the old threshold as templates, if possible. If the profile of the new threshold differs from the old threshold, trace the new profile onto the bottoms of the door stops. Chisel the stops to fit.

3 Apply caulk to the sill. Position the new threshold, pressing it into the caulk. Drive the screws provided with the threshold through the pre-drilled holes in the center channel, and into the sill. Install the threshold insert (see manufacturer's directions).

Tips for Weatherizing Doors

Patio door: Use rubber compression strips to seal the channels in patio door jambs, where movable panels fit when closed. Also install a patio door insulator kit (plastic sheeting installed similarly to plastic sheeting for windows—page 83) on the interior side of the door.

Garage door: Attach a new rubber sweep to the bottom, outside edge of the garage door if the old sweep has deteriorated. Also check the door jambs for drafts, and add weatherstripping, if needed.

Maintaining Storm Doors & Windows

Removable storm windows are excellent insulators when they are in good condition, and removable screens provide full ventilation. For these reasons, many homeowners still prefer them over combination storm and screen windows—even though they must be changed with the seasons.

Simple wood-sash construction and a lack of moving parts make removable storm and screen windows easy to repair and maintain. Replacing screening or glass, tightening loose joints, and applying fresh paint are the primary maintenance jobs.

Combination storm and screen windows offer convenience, and can be repaired simply if you have a little know-how and the right replacement parts.

Build a storage rack for removable screens and storm windows. Simply attach a pair of 2 × 4s to the rafters of your garage or the ceiling joists in your basement. Attach window-hanger hardware to the top rails of the screen and storm windows, if they do not already have them. Space the hangers uniformly. Then, attach screw eyes to the 2 × 4s in matching rows to fit the window hangers.

Tools & Materials

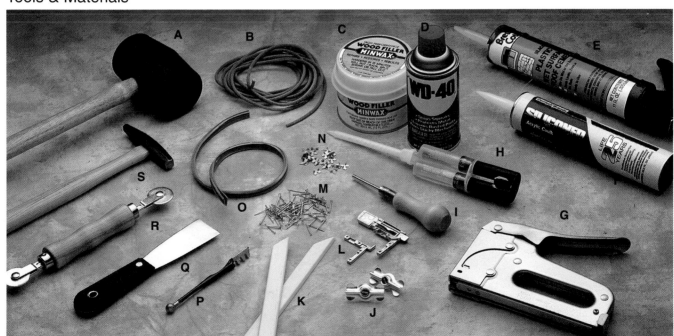

Tools and materials for repairing and maintaining storm windows include: rubber mallet (A), spline cord for metal sash (B), epoxy wood filler (C), penetrating lubricant (D), roof cement (E), siliconized acrylic caulk (F), staple gun (G), epoxy glue (H), brad pusher (I), turnbuttons (J), retaining strips for wood sash (K), metal sash replacement hardware (L), wire brads (M), glazier's points (N), rubber window gasket for metal sash (O), glass cutter (P), putty knife (Q), spline roller (R), tack hammer (S).

Tips for Maintaining Storm Doors & Windows

Tighten storm door latches by redriving loose screws in the strikeplate. If the latch does not catch on the strikeplate, loosen the screws on the strikeplate, insert thin wood shims between the plate and the jamb, and retighten the screws.

Add a wind chain if your storm door does not have one. Wind chains prevent doors from blowing open too far, causing damage to the door hinges or closer. Set the chain so the door will not open more than 90°.

Adjust the door closer so it has the right amount of tension to close the door securely, without slamming. Most closers have tension-adjustment screws at the end of the cylinder farther from the hinge side of the door.

Replace turnbuttons and window clips that do not hold storm windows tightly in place. Fill old screw holes with wood putty or toothpicks and glue before driving screws.

Lubricate sliding assemblies on metal-framed combination storm windows once a year, using penetrating lubricant.

Replace deteriorated glazing around glass panes in wood-framed windows. Sound glazing makes windows more energy-efficient and more attractive.

Repairing Wood Storm Windows & Screens

Because they are installed, removed, transported, and stored so frequently, removable wood storm windows need repair and maintenance regularly. Broken glass, torn screens, loose joints or hangers, dry or missing glazing, and failed paint are the primary problems. Fortunately, fixing wood storm windows is simple, and maintaining them well has a high payback in the appearance and efficiency of your house.

Everything You Need:

Tools: utility knife, clamps, drill, mallet, putty knife, staple gun, tack hammer, scissors.

Materials: epoxy glue, dowels, caulk, replacement glass, glazier's points, glazing compound, screening, wire brads.

Clean out recesses for glass and screening by carefully removing old glass, glazing compound, and glazier's points (or screening and retaining strips). Scrape residue from the recess with an old chisel, then paint with a coat of primer or sealer before installing new glass or screen.

How to Repair Loose Joints in Wood Sash Frames

1 Remove the glass or screening, then carefully separate the loose joint, using a flat pry bar if necessary. Scrape the mating surfaces clean. Inject epoxy glue into the joint (plain wood glue should not be used for exterior work). Press the mating surfaces back together and clamp with bar clamps, making sure the frame is square.

2 After the glue is dry, reinforce the repair by drilling two ⅜"-diameter holes through the joint (mortise-and-tenon joints are common). Cut two ⅜"-diameter dowels about 1" longer than the thickness of the frame, and round over one end of each dowel with sandpaper. Coat the dowels with epoxy glue, and drive them through the holes. After the glue dries, trim the ends of the dowels with a backsaw, then sand until they are flush with the sash. Touch up with paint.

How to Replace Glass in a Wood Storm Window

1 Clean and prepare the glass recess (top photo, previous page). Measuring from the outside shoulders of the glass recess, measure the full width and height of the opening, subtract ⅛" from each dimension, and have new glass cut to fit. Apply a thin bead of caulk in the recess to create a bed for the new pane of glass.

2 Press the new glass pane into the fresh caulk. Use a putty knife or screwdriver blade to push glazier's points into the frame every 8" to 10" to hold the glass in place.

3 Roll glazing compound into ⅜"-diameter "snakes" and press the snakes into the joint between the glass and the frame. Smooth the compound with a putty knife held at a 45° angle to create a flat surface. Strip off the excess. Let the compound dry for several days before painting.

How to Replace Screening in a Wood Storm Window

1 Completely clean and prepare the recess (top photo, previous page). Cut a new piece of screening at least 3" longer in height and in width than the opening. TIP: Use fiberglass screening for residential windows—it is easy to work with, and will not rust or corrode.

2 Tack the top edge of the screening into the recess with a staple gun. Stretch the screen tightly toward the bottom. Tack the bottom into the recess. Tack one side in place. Then, stretch the screening tightly across the frame, and tack the other side.

3 Attach retaining strips over the edges of the screening. Do not use old nail holes: drill ½₂"-diameter pilot holes in the retaining strips, then drive 1" wire brads. Trim off excess screening with a sharp utility knife.

Repairing Metal Storm Windows

Compared to removable wood storm windows, repairing combination storms is a little more complex. But there are several repairs you can make without too much difficulty, as long as you find the right parts. Bring the old corner keys, gaskets, or other original parts to a hardware store that repairs storm windows so the clerk can help you find the correct replacement parts (page 94, step 3). If you cannot find the right parts, have a new sash built.

Slide tab

Remove metal storm window sash by pressing in the release hardware in the lower rail (like the slide tabs above), then lifting the sash out. Sash hangers on the corners of the top rail (see step 2, next page) should be aligned with the notches in the side channels before removal.

Everything You Need:

Tools: tape measure, scissors, utility knife, spline roller, drill, screwdriver, hammer, nail set.

Materials: spline cord, rubber gasket, glass, screening, replacement hardware.

How to Replace Screening in a Metal Storm Window

1 Remove the spline cord holding the damaged screening in the frame. Also remove the old screening material, and clean any debris from the spline-cord tracks in the frame.

2 Cut the new screening material at least 3" wider and longer than the frame opening, and lay it over the frame. Set the spline cord over the screening so it is aligned with the spline-cord track.

3 At the top of the window, press the spline cord into the spline-cord track with a spline roller. Stretch the screening across the opening and continue setting the cord all the way around the frame. Trim off the excess screening with a utility knife.

How to Replace Glass in a Metal Storm Window

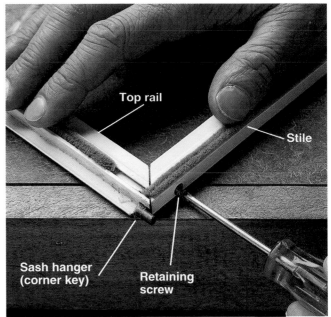

1 Remove the sash frame from the window, then completely remove the broken glass from the sash. Remove the rubber gasket that framed the old glass pane and remove any glass remnants. Find the dimensions for the replacement glass by measuring between the inside edges of the frame opening, then adding twice the thickness of the rubber gasket to each measurement.

2 Set the frame on a flat surface, and disconnect the top rail. Normally, you need to remove the retaining screws in the sides of the frame stiles where they join the top rail. After unscrewing the retaining screws, pull the top rail loose, pulling gently in a downward motion to avoid damaging the L-shaped corner keys that join the rail and the stiles. For glass replacement, you need only disconnect the top rail.

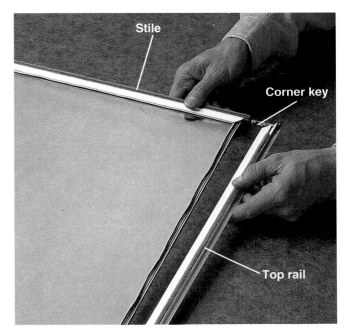

3 Fit the rubber gasket (buy a replacement if the original is in poor condition) around one edge of the replacement glass pane. At corners, cut the spine of the gasket partway so it will bend around the corner. Continue fitting the gasket around the pane, cutting at the corners, until all four edges are covered. Trim off any excess gasket material.

4 Slide the glass pane into the channels in the stiles and the bottom rail of the sash frame. Insert the corner keys into the top rail, then slip the other ends of the keys into the frame stiles. Press down on the top rail until the mitered corners are flush with the stiles. Drive the retaining screws back through the stiles and into the top rail to join the frame together. Insert the frame back into the window.

How to Disassemble & Repair a Metal Sash Frame

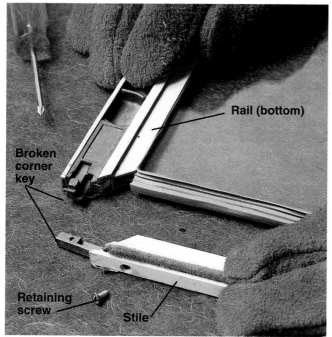

Rail (bottom)

Broken corner key

Retaining screw

Stile

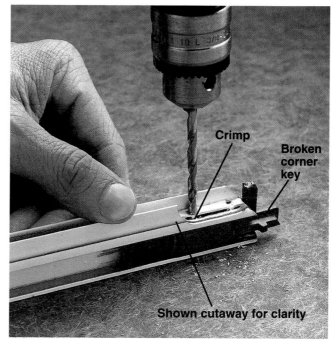

Crimp

Broken corner key

Shown cutaway for clarity

1 Metal window sash are held together at the corner joints by L-shaped pieces of hardware that fit into grooves in the sash frame pieces. To disassemble a broken joint, start by disconnecting the stile and rail at the broken joint—there is usually a retaining screw driven through the stile that must be removed.

2 Corner keys are secured in the rail slots with crimps that are punched into the metal over the key. To remove keys, drill through the metal in the crimped area, using a drill bit the same diameter as the crimp. Carefully knock the broken key pieces from the frame slots with a screwdriver and hammer.

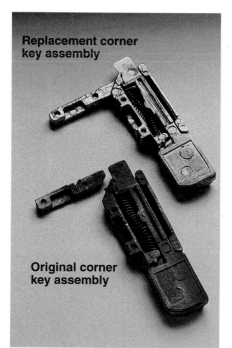

Replacement corner key assembly

Original corner key assembly

3 Locate matching replacement parts for the broken corner key (page 92), which is usually an assembly of two or three pieces. There are dozens of different types, so it is important that you save the old parts for reference.

4 Insert the replacement corner key assembly into the slot in the rail. Use a nail set as a punch, and rap it into the metal over the corner key, creating a new crimp to hold the key in place.

5 Insert the glass and gasket into the frame slots (see previous page), then reassemble the frame and drive in retainer screws (for screen windows, replace the screening).

Replacing Storm Windows

As old removable storm windows wear out, many homeowners elect to replace them with modern combination storm windows. Designed to mount permanently in the existing opening, "retrofit" combination storm windows are very easy to install, and fairly inexpensive.

Most retrofit storm windows attach to the outside edges of the window stops on the sides and top of the window opening. Most windows do not have a bottom stop. Secure the bottom rail of the new window with caulk. Common window sizes are stocked at most building centers, but you may need to order custom-made windows. Bring exact measurements (photo, right) when you order the windows. You also will be asked to choose a finish color and a style. If you have operating double-hung windows, choose 3-sash windows so you have the option of opening the top storm sash.

Everything You Need:

Tools: screwdriver, drill, tape measure.

Materials: replacement storm windows, caulk or panel adhesive, screws.

"Retrofit" storm windows attach to the window stops in the existing window opening. The easiest way to size them is to use the dimensions of old storms. Otherwise, measure the narrowest point between side jambs to find the width, and measure the shortest point from the header to the sill (where it meets the front edges of the stops) to find the height.

How to Install New Combination Storm Windows

1 Buy replacement storm windows to fit your window openings (photo, above). Test-fit windows before installing them. To install, first apply a bead of exterior-grade panel adhesive or caulk to the outside edges of the window stops at the top and sides.

2 Predrill pilot holes for fasteners in the mounting flanges, spaced 12" apart, making sure they will be centered over the stops. Press the new storm window into the opening, centered between the side stops, with the bottom rail resting on the window sill.

3 Drive fasteners (#4 × 1" sheet-metal screws work well), starting at the top. Make sure the window is squarely in the opening, then fill in the fasteners on the side stops. Apply caulk along the bottom rail, leaving a ¼"-wide gap midway to function as a weep hole.

Painting Your House

Painting your house yourself greatly reduces the cost and, if done with care and patience, the finished product will look as good as that produced by a professional contractor.

A house-painting project breaks naturally into two stages: preparing the surfaces, and applying the paint. In most cases, the preparation work is more time-consuming than the application. But the investment of time is reflected in an even and long-lasting painted finish.

Planning and timing are critical elements in a painting project. Try to tackle only one side of your house at a time. Scraping and sanding the old paint exposes your siding to the elements, which can cause wood pores to become plugged—resulting in a poor bond with the paint. Cover the siding with primer and paint as soon as you finish the preparation.

When applied correctly over a well-prepared, primed surface, paint can last 10 years or more, especially with regular maintenance. By touching up minor problems, like chips or localized flaking, you can prevent water from building up beneath the surface. Cracks and alligatoring should be sanded, primed, and painted as soon as they occur. Left uncorrected, they invite mildew formation, leading to staining and the eventual failure of the paint. Pressure washing your siding should be the cornerstone of your annual maintenance program.

Like any project that involves the use of ladders or scaffolding, painting your house requires good safety practices. Read the section on safety (pages 10 to 13) before you start.

This section shows:

Safety Warning:

Lead-based paint is a hazardous material: its handling and disposal are strictly regulated. Especially if your home was built before 1960, you should test the paint for lead using a lead-testing kit (available at building centers and paint stores). Call your local building inspector or waste management department for information on handling and disposing of lead paint.

Evaluating Painted Surfaces

Two primary factors work against painted surfaces: moisture and age. A simple leak or a failed vapor barrier inside the house can ruin even the most carefully executed paint job. If you notice signs of paint failure, like blistering or peeling, take action to correct the problem right away. If the damage to the surface is caught in time, you may be able to correct it with just a little bit of touch-up painting.

Evaluating the painted surfaces of your house can help you identify problems with siding, trim, roofs, and moisture barriers. Before you begin a thorough inspection of the painted surfaces, read pages 6 to 9 and the evaluation information at the beginning of each section in this book.

Check sheltered areas first. Initial signs of paint failure in areas that receive little or no direct sunlight are a warning sign that neighboring areas may be in danger of similar paint failure.

Common Forms of Paint Failure

Blistering describes paint that bubbles on the surface. It is an early sign that more serious problems, like peeling, may be forming.

Causes: Blistering can result from poor preparation or hasty application of primer or paint. The blisters are caused by trapped moisture as it forces its way through the surface.

Solution: Scrape and touch up localized blistering. For widespread damage, remove paint down to bare wood, then apply new primer and paint.

Peeling occurs when paint disengages entirely from the surface, falling away in flakes.

Causes: Peeling is most often associated with persistent moisture problems, generally from a leak or a failed vapor barrier.

Solution: Identify and correct any moisture problems. If the peeling is localized, scrape and sand the damaged area only, then touch up with new primer and paint. If peeling is widespread, remove the old paint down to bare wood. Apply new primer and paint.

Alligatoring is widespread flaking and cracking of surfaces, typically seen on old paint and surfaces with many built-up layers of paint.

Causes: Alligatoring can be caused by excessive layers of paint, inadequate surface preparation, or insufficient drying time for a primer.

Solution: Repainting will not permanently cover significant alligatoring. Remove the old paint down to bare wood, then prime and repaint.

Detecting the Source of Moisture Beneath a Painted Surface

Localized blistering and peeling indicates that moisture, usually from a leaky roof or gutter system, is trapped under the paint. Check roofing and gutter materials to find the source of the leak. Also look for leaking pipes inside the wall. Correct the moisture problem before you repaint.

Clearly defined blistering and peeling occurs when a humid room, like a bathroom, has an insufficient vapor barrier (page 76). If there is a clear line where an interior wall ends, you probably will need to remove the wall coverings and replace the vapor barrier. In some cases, you may be able to solve the problem by increasing ventilation or adding a dehumidifier.

Identifying Common Surface Problems

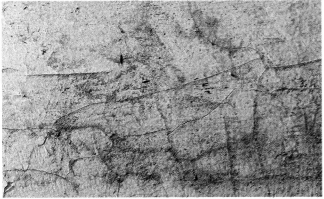

Mildew forms in cracks and in humid areas that receive little direct sunlight. Wash the areas with a 1:1 solution of household chlorine bleach and water, or with trisodium phosphate (TSP) to kill the mildew.

Rust occurs when moisture penetrates failed paint on iron or steel. Remove the rust and any loose paint with a wire brush attachment and portable drill, then prime and repaint the affected area.

Bleeding spots occur when nails in siding "pop" and turn rusty. Remove the nails, sand out the rust, and drive in new ring-shank siding nails. Apply metal primer, then paint to blend in.

Efflorescence occurs in masonry when minerals leech through the surface, forming a crystalline or powdery layer. Use muriatic acid to remove efflorescence before priming and painting.

Materials for painting include: tarps, masking tape, sandpaper, caulk, primers (tinted to match paint color), house paint, trim paint, and special-task paints.

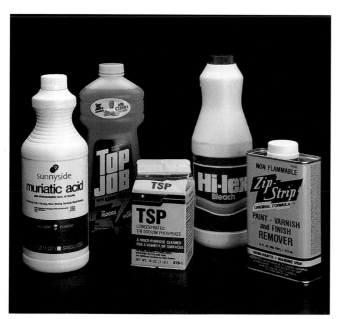

Chemicals and cleaners for paint maintenance and for surface preparation include (from left): muriatic acid for cleaning rust from metal, household detergent and TSP (trisodium phosphate) for general washing of surfaces, household chlorine bleach for cleaning mildew, and chemical stripper for removing thick layers of paint from delicate surfaces.

Tools & Materials

An investment in quality primer and house paint will make your hard work last for years longer than if you use cheaper products. High-quality preparation and application tools are also a good investment because they produce better results with less work.

Traditionally, almost all house paint was oil-based. But new latex-based products now rival oil-based products in durability and appearance, without the hazards, odors, and disposal problems of oil-based paints.

How to Estimate Your Paint Needs

Add:
square footage of walls (length × height)
square footage of soffit panels
15% allowance for waste
Subtract:
square footage of doors and windows

Find the coverage rate on the labels of the paint you will use (350 square feet per gallon is an average rate). Divide the total square footage by the coverage rate to determine the number of gallons you will need for each coat.

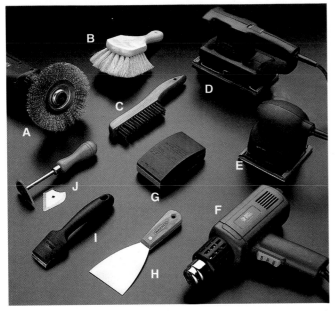

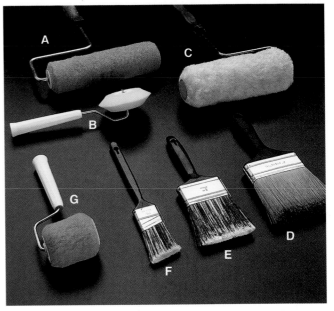

Tools for paint removal include: drill with wire-wheel attachment (A), stiff-bristled scrub brush (B), wire brush (C), ⅓-sheet finishing sander (D), ¼-sheet finishing sander (E), heat gun (F), sanding block (G), putty knife (H), paint scraper (I), and detail scraper with interchangeable heads (J).

Tools for applying paint include: roller and sleeve with ⅜" nap for smooth or semi-smooth surfaces (A), corner roller for corners and trim (B), roller with ⅝" nap for rough surfaces (C), 4" paint brush for lap siding (D), 3" paint brush for siding and trim (E), 2" sash brush for trim and window frames (F), 3"-wide roller for painting trim (G). NOTE: All brushes shown have synthetic bristles for use with latex-based paint.

Rent a pressure washer and attachments for the surface-preparation process. A pressure washer cleans siding thoroughly, and removes old, flaky paint. A nozzle with an extension pole attaches to the hose from the pressure washer. Accessories, like the rotating scrub brush shown, clean hard-to-reach areas.

Sanded to bare wood

Scraped and spot-sanded

Pressure-washed only

Preparation defines the final appearance. For the smoothest finish, sand all the way to bare wood with a power sander (top). For a less time-consuming (but rougher) finish, scrape off loose paint, then spot-sand the rough edges (middle). Pressure-washing alone removes some flaky paint, but it will not create a satisfactory finish (bottom).

Preparing Surfaces for Paint

Preparing the surface is a crucial part of the house-painting process. Generally, the more preparation work you do, the smoother and more long-lasting the finished surface will be. But anyone who paints his or her house learns quickly that there is a point of diminishing return when it comes to preparation. You must decide for yourself how much sanding and scraping is enough for you to obtain a finish that meets your demands. But whether you are attempting to create a glass-smooth finish with a professional look or you simply want to freshen up the look of your house, always remove and spot-sand all paint that has lost its bond with the surface.

Everything You Need:

Tools: pressure washer, paint scrapers, finishing sander, wire brush, stiff-bristled brush, file, sanding blocks, hammer, putty knife.

Materials: sandpaper, epoxy wood filler, caulk, colored push pins, tape.

Tips for Pressure-washing

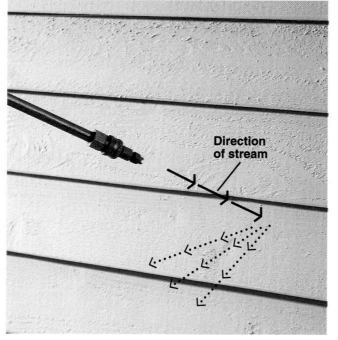

Direction of stream

Direct the water stream at a downward angle when pressure-washing siding. Avoid getting too close to the surface with the sprayer head, because the force of the stream can damage siding and trim. When pressure-washing high on the wall, use an extension attachment (page 101).

Attach a rotating scrub brush attachment to clean hard-to-reach areas, like cornices and soffits. Check with the rental store for available pressure-washer accessories.

Tips for Protecting Your House & Yard

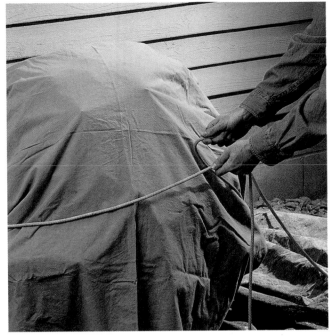

Protect delicate plants and shrubs with tarps when you are working near them. Also lay tarps on the ground around your house to collect debris. Turn off air conditioners and other appliances, and cover them with plastic sheets to protect them from debris and paint.

Remove shutters and decorative trim to protect them from damage and to give you better access to the surface of your house. Inspect the shutters and trim to see if they are in good repair, and fix them if necessary (pages 68 to 69). Prepare, prime, and paint them before reinstalling.

Options for Removing Paint

Use a heat gun to loosen thick layers of paint. Aim the gun at the surface, and move it constantly. Follow with a scraper once the paint releases. Read the manufac-turer's directions and precautions.

Use chemical stripper to remove paint from delicate trim. Work in a well-ventilated area, wearing heavy-duty rubber gloves. Read the stripper manufacturer's direc-tions and precautions.

Rent a siding sander to remove large areas of paint on wood lap siding. Rent a sander with a disk the same diameter as the width of the reveal area on your siding. Get instructions from the rental store.

How to Prepare Surfaces for Paint

1 Pressure-wash your house (page 102). Pressure-washing cleans the surface and dislodges loose paint. Allow the house to dry thoroughly before continuing with the preparation work.

2 Scrape off loose paint that was not removed during pressure-washing, using a paint scraper. Be careful not to damage the surface with overly aggressive scraping.

3 Remove loose paint in hard-to-reach areas with detail scrapers (available at building centers and woodworker's stores). Some have interchangeable heads that match common trim profiles.

4 Use a finishing sander with 80-grit sandpaper to smooth out rough paint.

5 Use sanding blocks and 80 to 120-grit sandpaper to remove paint and smooth out ridges in hard-to-reach areas of trim. Sanding blocks are available at building centers in a variety of shapes and sizes, like the teardrop design shown here. Or, you can make your own blocks from dowels, wood scraps, garden hose, or other household materials.

6 Inspect all surfaces for cracks, rot, or other damage. Mark damaged areas with colored push pins or tape so you can locate them easily when making repairs.

7 Repair all the damaged areas (pages 60 to 64 and 68 to 69).

8 Use a finishing sander with 120-grit sandpaper to sand down ridges and hard edges left from the scraping process, creating a smooth surface. Also sand repaired areas.

(continued next page)

How to Prepare Surfaces for Paint (continued)

9 Scuff-sand glossy surfaces on doors, window casings, and any surfaces painted with enamel paint, using a coarse abrasive pad or 150-grit sandpaper. Scuffing creates a better bonding surface for primer and paint.

10 Fill cracks in siding and gaps around window and door trim with paintable siliconized acrylic caulk. The caulk makes a tight, long-lasting seal.

Tips for Removing Clear Finishes

Pressure-wash stained or unpainted surfaces that have been treated with a wood preservative or protectant (page 102) before recoating with fresh sealant. Clear topcoats and sealants can flake and peel, just like paint.

Use a stiff-bristled brush to dislodge any flakes of loosened surface coating not removed by pressure-washing. Do not use a wire brush on wood surfaces.

Tips for Removing Paint from Metal & Masonry

Use a wire brush to remove loose paint and rust from metal hardware, like railings and ornate trim. Cover the surface with metal primer immediately after brushing to prevent new rust from forming.

Scuff-sand metal siding and trim with medium-coarse steel wool or a coarse abrasive pad. Wash the surface before priming and painting.

Use a drill with a wire-wheel attachment to remove loose mortar, mineral deposits, or paint from mortar lines in masonry surfaces. Clean broad, flat surfaces with a wire brush. Correct any minor damage with masonry repair products (pages 118 to 119).

Remove rust from metal hardware with diluted muriatic acid solution. CAUTION: When working with muriatic acid, wear safety equipment, work in a well-ventilated area, and follow the manufacturer's directions and precautions.

Paint downward from the top of your house, covering as much surface as you can reach comfortably without moving your ladder or scaffolding. After the primer or paint dries, return to each section and touch up any unpainted areas that were covered by the pads of the ladder or ladder stabilizer.

Applying Primer & Paint

Like doing preparation work, applying primer and paint requires good planning and execution. If you use a quality primer that is tinted to match the color of your house paint as closely as possible, you can often achieve good coverage with only one coat of house paint.

Keep an eye on the weather when you are planning to paint. Damp weather or rain that falls within an hour or two of application will ruin your paint job. Do not apply paint when the temperature is below 50°F, or above 90°F. And avoid working during high winds—it is unsafe, and dust and dirt are likely to blow onto the freshly painted surface.

TIP: Apply primer and paint in the shade or in indirect sunlight. Direct sunlight dries primers and paints too rapidly, causing moisture to become trapped below the dried surface. This can result in blistering, peeling, and other types of paint failure. Also, lap marks and brush marks are more likely to show up if paint is applied in direct sunlight.

Tips for Applying Primer & Paint

Use the best type of primer or paint for the job. For best results, use a metal primer with rust inhibitor for metal surfaces, and use masonry primer with an anti-chalking additive for masonry surfaces. Always read the manufacturer's recommendations for use.

Follow a logical painting sequence. For example, priming and painting wood stairs and porch floors *after* walls, doors, and trim prevents the need to touch up spills.

Options for Applying Primer & Paint

Use paint brushes for maximum control of the materials. Have clean 4" and 2½" or 3" brushes on hand, as well as a tapered sash brush (page 101). Using brushes that fit the area helps you create a professional-looking finish.

Use paint rollers to paint smooth surfaces quickly. Use a roller with an 8" or 9" roller sleeve (top) for broad surfaces. Use a 3"-wide roller to paint flat-surfaced trim, like end caps (bottom).

Use a power sprayer to apply paint to porch railings, ornate trim, shutters, and other hard-to-paint metal hardware. Read the manufacturer's directions before you start. NOTE: Professional-quality airless sprayers can be rented for large spray-painting projects.

Tips for Painting with a Paint Brush

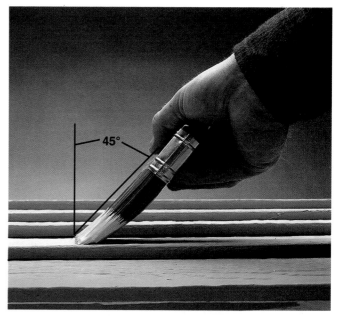

Load your paint brush with the correct amount of paint for the area you are painting. Use a full load for broad areas, a moderate load for smaller areas and feathering strokes, and a light load when painting or working around trim.

Hold the paint brush at a 45° angle when painting broad, flat areas. Apply just enough downward pressure to flex the bristles and "squeeze" the paint out of the brush. Load your brush properly (photo, left), use good brushing technique, and avoid overbrushing to achieve smooth, pleasing results.

How to Apply Paint to Flat Surfaces

1 Load your paint brush with a full load of paint. Starting at one end of the surface, make a long, smooth stroke until the paint begins to "feather" out.

2 As you finish the stroke, lift the brush gradually from the surface so you do not leave a definite ending point. If the paint appears uneven or contains heavy brush marks, smooth it out with the brush. Be careful to avoid overbrushing.

3 Reload your brush and make another stroke from the other direction, painting over the feathered end of the first stroke to create a smooth, even surface. If the area where the two strokes meet is noticeable, rebrush it with a light load of paint. Feather out the starting point of the second stroke to avoid lap marks.

Tips for Working with Paint

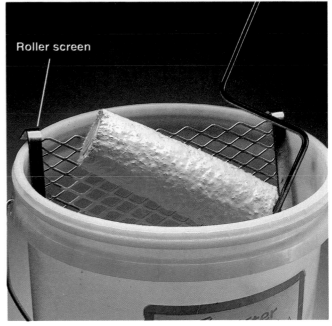

Mix cans of paint together, called boxing, in a large bucket. Stir thoroughly with a stir stick or paint-stirring attachment for your power drill. This ensures that the paint is uniform in color. Pour the mixed paint back into the cans after it is blended (if you are painting with a paint brush). If you are painting with a roller, leave the paint in the larger container.

Use a roller screen inside a five-gallon paint bucket when painting with a roller. Before starting, wet the roller nap with water (if using latex-based paint), then squeeze out any excess water. Dip the roller in the paint, and roll back and forth across the roller screen. The roller sleeve should be full, but not dripping, when lifted from the container.

Tips for Cleaning Painting Tools

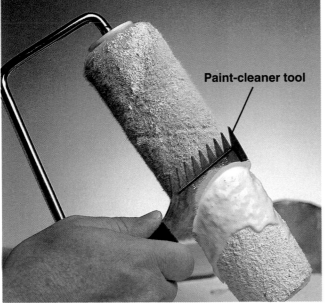

Clean roller sleeves with the curved side of a paint-cleaner tool. Remove as much paint as possible, then clean the roller with a solution of warm water and household soap. Continue squeezing paint and water solution from the roller with the cleaning tool until all of the paint is removed. Rinse thoroughly and hang roller sleeves to dry.

Clean paint brushes in a solution of warm water and dish soap (for latex-based paints—use paint thinner for oil-based paints). Rinse thoroughly, then comb the bristles of the brush with the spiked edge of a paint-cleaner tool (photo, left).

How to Apply Primer & Paint to Your House

Of all the steps involved in painting your house, applying paint is perhaps the most satisfying. Prime all surfaces to be painted, then go back and apply the paint. Allow ample drying time for primers before applying paint.

If you use quality primer that is tinted in the color range of your house paint or trim paint, you should get sufficent paint coverage with just one coat.

Everything You Need:

Tools: 4" paint brush, 2½" or 3" paint brush, sash brush, scaffolding or ladder.

Materials: primers, house paint, trim paint, cleanup materials.

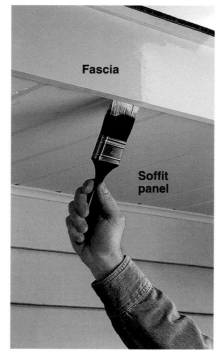

1 Paint the face of the fascia first, then cut in paint at the bottom edges of soffit panels. NOTE: Fascia and soffits are usually painted the same color as the trim.

TIP: Paint gutters and downspouts after painting the fascia, beginning with the back sides and working toward the front. If you use metal primer, you can paint gutters and downspouts with trim paint.

2 Paint the soffit panels and trim with a 4" paint brush. Start by cutting in around the edges of the panels using the narrow edge of the brush, then feather in the broad surfaces of the soffit panels with full loads of paint. Make sure to get good coverage in the groove areas.

TIP: Paint any decorative trim near the top of the house at the same time you paint soffits and fascia. Use a 2½" or 3" paint brush for broader surfaces, and use a sash brush for more intricate trim areas.

3 Paint the bottom edges of lap siding with the paint brush held flat against the wall. Paint the bottom edges of several siding pieces before returning to paint the faces of the siding boards.

4 Paint the broad faces of the siding boards with a 4" brush. Use the painting technique shown on page 110. Working down from the top, paint only as much surface as you can reach comfortably.

5 Paint all the siding all the way down to the foundation, working from top to bottom. Shift the ladder or scaffolding, and paint the next section. NOTE: Paint up to the edges of end caps and window and door trim that will be painted later. If trim will not be painted, mask it off or use a paint shield.

VARIATION: On board-and-batten or any vertical-panel siding, paint the edges of the battens or top boards first. Paint the faces of the battens before the sides dry, then paint the large, broad surfaces between the battens, feathering in at the edges of the battens. Rollers are good tools for panel siding (use a ⅝"-nap sleeve for rough-textured panels).

(continued next page)

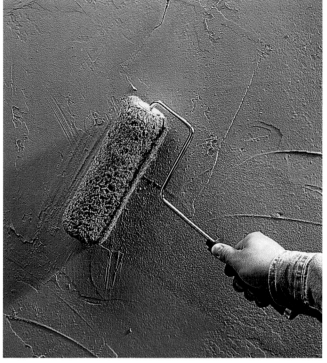

VARIATION: On stucco siding, paint the walls with a paint roller and ⅝"-nap sleeve. Use a 3" trim roller or a 3" paint brush for trim.

6 Paint the foundation with anti-chalking masonry primer. Start by cutting in the areas around basement windows. Then, paint the broad surfaces of the foundation with a 4" brush, working the paint into any mortar lines.

7 Paint doors and windows, using a sash brush. Follow the correct sequence: First, paint the beveled edges of raised door panels, and the insides of muntins or frames on windows; next, paint the faces of the door panels before the edges dry; next, paint rails (horizontal frame members) on doors and windows; last, paint the faces of the stiles (vertical frame members).

8 Use a trim brush or sash brush and a moderate load of paint to paint the inside edges of door and window jambs, casings, and brick molding. NOTE: The surfaces on the interior side of the door stop usually match the color of the interior trim.

9 Paint the outside edges of casings and brick molding, using a sash brush (mask off freshly painted siding after it has dried).

10 Paint the faces of door jambs, casings, and brick molding, feathering fresh paint around the painted edges.

11 Paint wooden door thresholds and porch floors. Use specially-formulated enamel floor paint for maximum durability.

Protecting & Maintaining Your Home

Maintenance and protection work hand-in-hand to keep your house safe and attractive, and to lessen the likelihood that you will need to make major repairs. Exterior house maintenance can include a wide range of activities, from cleaning siding and trim once a year to touching up minor paint problems and making small repairs. In a very real sense, creating and following a comprehensive maintenance schedule is one of the most important ways to protect your house.

Other forms of house protection go beyond maintenance to include activities like pestproofing and improving security. By securing your house against pest infestation and against intruders, you will increase your ability to relax and enjoy your home.

In the first four sections of this book, we have shown you detailed information about repairing common problems that afflict the exterior of your house. Refer to these sections when making the minor repairs that are a part of any home main-tenance plan. Also refer to pages 118 to 119 for additional information on making quick repairs to concrete surfaces.

This section shows:

* Quick Fixes for Concrete & Asphalt (pages 118 to 119)
* Pestproofing Your Home (pages 120 to 121)
* Improving Home Security (pages 122 to 125)

Tips for Protecting & Maintaining Your Home

* Keep foundation plantings and tree limbs trimmed back so they are well clear of your house. They can cause damage, and they obscure entry points to your home, making it more inviting to intruders.
* Check weatherstripping around windows and doors before every heating season (pages 71 to 87).
* If you own a pressure-washer, use it to wash your siding at least once a year. Otherwise, use a garden hose and spray nozzle, scrubbing with mild detergent to remove heavy dirt buildup.

Tips for Exterior Home Maintenance

Follow a preventative maintenance schedule for the exterior of your home. The schedule should include tasks like cleaning the chimney flue (left) and cleaning out downspouts (right). Clean chimney flues with a chimney brush that fits the inside dimension of your chimney flue. Use a plumber's snake to remove clogs in downspouts. Also clean debris from gutters with an old kitchen spatula.

Quick Fixes for Concrete & Asphalt

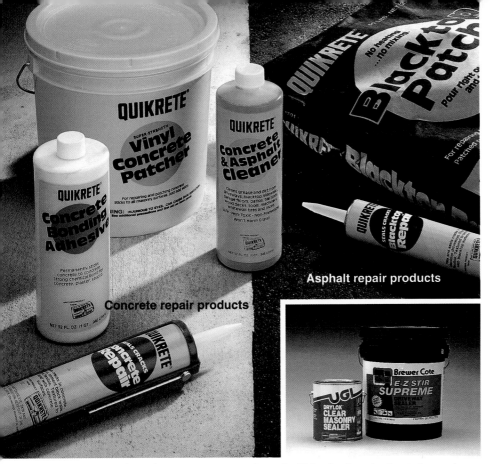

Asphalt repair products

Concrete repair products

Repair materials for concrete and asphalt include: vinyl-reinforced concrete patching compound, concrete bonding adhesive, gray-tinted concrete repair caulk, concrete/asphalt cleaner, asphalt patching compound, and asphalt repair caulk. Protective sealants (inset) include: clear masonry sealer and asphalt sealer.

You do not need years of experience working with asphalt, concrete, and brick to make effective repairs to masonry surfaces around your house. New lines of quick-fix repair products are designed to be used by any homeowner with a masonry problem.

Most concrete and asphalt repair products can be applied directly from the container, eliminating worry about mixing ratios and curing times. When surface preparation is required, it is usually only small amounts of scraping and cleaning.

Tips for Cleaning Concrete & Asphalt

Remove loose material from the damaged area, using a cold chisel. Also scrub with a wire brush, then wipe with water or concrete cleaning solution to remove residue.

Clean surfaces thoroughly before applying sealants or other repair products. Scrub stained areas with commercial asphalt or concrete cleaner and a brush, or use a solution of warm water and mild detergent for surfaces that are not heavily soiled.

Tips for Fixing Cracks

Concrete: Scrape and clean the crack (previous page), deepening the crack slightly. Overfill the crack slightly with gray-tinted concrete repair caulk. Smooth out with a putty knife, level with the surface.

Asphalt: Clean and repair using the same technique used for concrete (previous photo). Use asphalt repair caulk instead of concrete repair caulk.

Tips for Using Patching Products

Concrete: Prepare and clean damaged area (previous page), then apply a coat of bonding adhesive to the surface. Let the adhesive dry. Trowel a ¼"-thick layer of vinyl-reinforced concrete patching compound into the repair area. Let dry. Add more ¼"-thick layers until the patch is level with the surface, then trowel smooth.

Asphalt: Scrape and clean the damaged area (previous page), then pack the hole with loose asphalt patching material (overfill slightly). Warm the material carefully with a heat gun, then tamp and smooth out with a trowel until the repair is level with the surrounding surface.

Tips for Sealing Concrete & Asphalt

Concrete: Use clear masonry sealer on driveways or garage floors if you are having serious staining problems. Also apply it to exposed aggregate ("seeded") surfaces to help keep aggregate from popping out. Clean the surface thoroughly (previous page), then apply a thin coat of sealer with a ⅜"-nap paint roller.

Asphalt: Asphalt sealer gives a fresh, new appearance to old asphalt driveways. Repair any cracks and holes (photos above), then pour a pool of sealer on one corner of the surface. Spread into a thin layer with squeegee, covering the entire surface.

Pestproofing Your Home

Keeping pests out of your house is an ongoing battle you can win by taking some simple measures. Combating pests is mostly a matter of prompt detection and choosing the remedy best suited to the specific pests.

To detect pest problems, look for signs of entry around your house—especially holes or gaps near roof eaves, screenless or damaged vent covers, and cracks in foundations. Also look for tell-tale signs of infestation, like droppings or nesting materials. If the problem appears large in scale, or you are unsure how to address it, call an exterminator or a local agricultural extension agent.

Add a chimney cap to keep birds, bats, insects, and squirrels out of your chimney. A metal chimney cap with a cover and screening, sized to fit your flue, also sheds rainwater. Most chimney caps slip over the flue, and are held in place by fasteners or compression strips. Some chimney covers can impede air movement in the chimney or furnace—read the manufacturer's recommendations.

Tips for Identifying Infestation Problems

Look for anthills, tunnels, hives, and nests around the outside of your house. Finding their living quarters is a sure way to identify pests. Block off access points to your house near the nesting areas. For safety, use care when removing nests or hives, and avoid using chemical pesticides except as a last resort.

Examine moist areas in basements or garages for pests or signs of pest infestation, like droppings or nesting materials. Moisture attracts a host of crawling insects. If you have a minor moisture problem, try installing a dehumidifier. For major leaks, especially in foundations, call a building contractor or inspector.

Tips for Pestproofing Your House

Install protected dryer vents to help keep pests from entering your home. Because they are often warm, dryer vents are very attractive entry points, especially for small rodents. Protected dryer vents, sold at most building supply stores, are designed to be one-for-one replacements for standard flap-style vents (inset). They also help reduce energy loss.

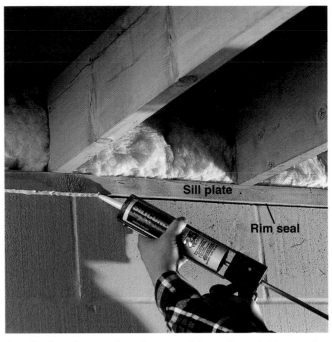

Caulk the rim seal at the top of your foundation wall (inside your basement). This is a prime entry spot for crawling insects. From outside, stuff caulking backer rope in any gaps between the siding and the foundation (page 81).

Replace damaged screening in windows and over air vent covers, using new insect screen (a 1/16" mesh). **CAUTION:** Do not use insect mesh to replace coarser screening on vent covers, unless you add another vent (pages 52 to 53) to compensate for lost air flow.

Look for signs of termite damage, like the characteristic tunnels they leave in wood. Termites are a very serious threat to any home. If you suspect that you have a problem, call a reputable exterminator immediately. You can purchase anti-termite chemicals, but most are difficult and dangerous to apply.

Framing members

Door jamb

Replace short hinge and lock screws with longer screws (3" or 4"), that extend through the door jamb and into framing members. This helps resist door kick-ins. Some standard hinge and lock screws are ½" to 1" long and extend only into the door jamb, making doors vulnerable to kick-ins.

Option: Install a Security Alarm System

At some time or another, most homeowners are tempted to install a security alarm system. There is some evidence that alarm systems are an effective way to deter intruders. Professionally installed systems that contact emergency operators automatically can save valuable time in dispatching emergency vehicles to your home. But alarm systems can be expensive to install and maintain, and more inexpensive models are prone to sending false alarms (which can mean substantial fines in some areas). If you are considering installing a security alarm system, first discuss your situation with a community officer from your local law enforcement agency.

Options for security alarm systems include:

Professionally installed alarm systems: Professional technicians will visit your home and work with you to decide what type of system best fits your needs. They will install and maintain the equipment. Most professionally installed systems will automatically relay the information to the appropriate emergency department if the alarm is tripped. Initial installation costs vary, but can be fairly expensive. Monthly service fees usually are charged.

Owner-installed systems: Many manufacturers sell security alarm systems designed to be installed and maintained by the homeowner. They vary from one or two simple sensors linked to a loud alarm horn, to fairly complex systems of sensors, alarms, and radio transmitters that often are wired into the electrical system in your house. Consult with a security professional, comparison shop, and do not skimp on quality.

Improving Home Security

There is a lot more to home security than simply keeping intruders out. Making a few security-minded improvements to your home has a great impact on how well you enjoy your home and surroundings: it creates peace of mind. Many security improvements also improve general safety around your house: for example, adding a motion-detector light above a door not only warns off intruders, it also improves visibility after dark for your family members.

Making your home uninviting to intruders is the primary objective of home security. Aim your home security improvements at deterrence and detection. If a potential intruder determines that he will have to gain entry by making noise or working in an area visible from the street, he will probably move on to another target.

Pay special attention to your doors—according to some estimates, more than 80% of all forced entries occur through them. Get in the habit of keeping doors and windows locked. Make sure every entry door in your home is equipped with a deadbolt lock.

For more information on home security, check with your local police department. Most will be happy to help.

Everything You Need:

Tools: screwdriver, circuit tester, electrical tape, connector caps, hammer, circular saw, nail set.

Materials: motion-detector light, 2 × 4 lumber, plywood shims, nails, screws.

Tips for Improving Security Lighting

Timer switch

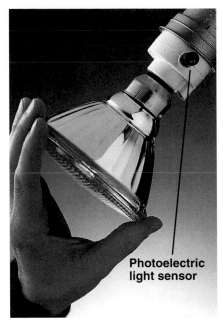

Photoelectric light sensor

Add new exterior lighting near entrances and garages. Security lights (even motion-detector lights) are available in a wide range of styles that are both functional and attractive.

Install timer switches to turn several lights on and off automatically. If you are often away from your house for extended periods of time, look for timer switches with random switching ability.

Install photo sensitive lights in your ordinary exterior light fixture. Photo sensitive lights turn on automatically at dusk, and turn off at dawn. Many are threaded so they can be screwed into a light fixture.

How to Replace an Exterior Light with a Motion-Detector Light

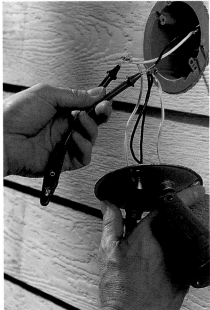

1 Shut off the power at your main circuit panel, and disconnect the old fixture. Carefully remove the mounting plate for your old light, then unscrew the wire nuts. Test the wire leads with a neon circuit tester. Do not proceed until you are sure the power is off.

2 Connect the wires for the new fixture, using wire nuts, and following the light manufacturer's directions. Secure the mounting plate to the electrical box. TIP: Test the motion detector to make sure it works correctly, then finish the installation by attaching the mounting plate.

3 Adjust the motion sensor for maximum coverage of entry points to your home. Select a setting so the sensor can detect motion well beyond the entry point, but not so far away that it reaches into traffic areas, like alleys (which will cause the light to turn on frequently, minimizing its impact).

How to Secure a Door Frame

1 Test the frame to find out if it needs shoring up—a loose door frame is much easier for an intruder to pry open. To test the frame, cut a 2 × 4 about 1" longer than the door width. Wedge the board between the jambs, near the lockset. If the frame flexes more than about ¼", proceed to step 2.

2 Remove the interior jamb casing so you can inspect the shims between the jambs and the framing members. Measure the gap, then cut plywood shims from material the same thickness as the gaps. Insert the plywood between the existing shims.

3 Drive 10d casing nails through the jambs and shims, and into the framing members. Set the nail heads, and reattach the casing.

Tips for Securing Doors

 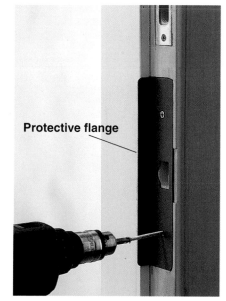 

Add metal sleeves to door edges around locksets and deadbolts to help prevent door kick-ins. Make sure the sleeves are the correct thickness for your door.

Add heavy-duty strike plates to reinforce your door and locks, and to help defeat kick-ins, jimmying, and prying. Some strike plates also have a flange that protects the lockset from jimmying and prying.

Install a wide-angle viewer in entry doors to allow you to see outside. Drill an eye-level hole the same diameter as the shaft of the viewer through the door. Insert the shaft so the attached eyepiece is flush against the door. Screw the exterior eyepiece onto the shaft.

Tips for Securing Windows

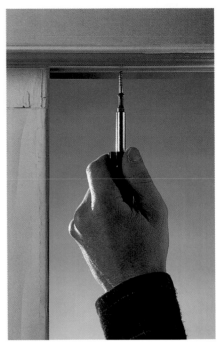

Pin sliding sashes together with ¼" x 3" eyehole bolts. With the window closed, drill a ¼"-diameter x 1¾"-deep hole, at a slight angle, through the top rail of the bottom sash and into the bottom rail of the top sash. This forces intruders to break the glass to gain entry.

Block sash tracks on sliding windows and doors by wedging a board or thick dowel between the inside (movable) frame and the door or window jamb.

Drive a screw into the top channel of side-by-side sliding windows or patio doors. This keeps intruders from lifting window sash or door panels out of their tracks to gain entry. Make sure the screw does not interfere with the normal operation of the sliding sash or panel.

Install protective bars or gates on the interior of ground-level windows to prevent entry. Swinging gates can be latched shut from the inside, so they may be opened easily in an emergency. Never install permanent obstructions in windows.

Remove crank handles from opening mechanisms on awning and casement windows. This forces intruders to climb through a frame filled with broken glass, instead of simply cranking open the window after it breaks. Create a permanent storage spot for the handle, at least an arm's length from the window.

INDEX

Cy DeCosse Incorporated offers a variety of how-to books. For information write:
  Cy DeCosse Subscriber Books
  5900 Green Oak Drive
  Minnetonka, MN 55343